Out of the Mouth of Babes!

Christian Witnessing Tools with a Twist

C.C. Houghton

authorHOUSE®

AuthorHouse™
1663 Liberty Drive
Bloomington, IN 47403
www.authorhouse.com
Phone: 1 (800) 839-8640

Published by AuthorHouse 09/07/2018

ISBN: 978-1-5462-5849-0 (sc)
ISBN: 978-1-5462-5848-3 (e)

Library of Congress Control Number: 2018910621

Print information available on the last page.

Scripture taken from The Holy Bible, King James Version. Public Domain

The Terrible Parable of the Defective Afghan

I while back I worked months and months making an afghan. I finished the last stitches with a flourish and proudly spread it out to have a good look at it and thought, "What a beautiful piece of work!" Then I saw it!! A WHOLE SECTION of the pattern had been left out! Depression city!

I showed the defective finished product to my husband, Doug, all the while groaning and moaning about how awful it looked. Doug looked and looked... and couldn't see anything missing at ALL. He kept muttering, "I don't see anything wrong...I don't see anything wrong." (But then, this is the same man who didn't see the edge of a roof either! See the end of this Parable for an explanation of that.)

But a whole section WAS missing; the afghan was complete and I couldn't fix it. If I wanted a perfect afghan I'd have to start over again and put in ALL the sections. End of pitiful story.

So what's my point already? I realized the situation was a picture of Doug's and my physical births the way God saw it—Doug's many years ago and mine many, MANY years ago. Every good story starts out, "Once upon a time..." so...........

Once upon a time, Doug and I were both born physically after nine long months of growing in the dark. FINALLY, we were completely formed and were born with a FLOURISH! Our human parents beamed and said, "What a beautiful piece of work!! Fingers and toes all intact. Perfect!"

However, the first thing God saw when He looked at us—other than how cute we were—was that there was a WHOLE SECTION missing in both of us! The Spirit Section just wasn't there. God shook His head and said: "Sheesh! These human models ALWAYS end up short the Spirit Section. What a pain! Now they've gotta go through MY birth process if they're EVER going to get the Spirit inserted. These humans just NEVER turn out right on their own!"

1

Well, God started working on my "spiritual pregnancy" as soon as He could. He knew a tough job when He saw one. He had my parents trundle me off to Sunday School when I was just little and I learned all the Bible stories–but no real faith that Christ had died for me sank in. When I was older, my sister-in-law told me things about the Book of Revelation that really interested me. She gave me Christian tracts too, saying I needed to be "reborn," but I ignored them because I was perfectly good the way I was...went to church every Sunday...TAUGHT Sunday School. I liked me FINE!

In desperation to get me through the "pregnancy" stage, the Lord moved me to Michigan and plopped me down four houses away from a lady who became my friend. We had a lot of conversations about the Bible and I started going to Bible study with her and started learning things–and they were actually INTERESTING! One day she said, "If you were the only person ever born on this earth, would Christ have had to die just for you?" I said, "Yes, I've always believed that..." but for the FIRST time light dawned and I realized that was true. After 28 years of "growing in the dark," I was "born again" at that moment–born a second time–spiritually–simply by believing and understanding what Christ had freely done for me. God wiped His brow and said, "FINALLY! Some of these humans are certainly slow-growing specimens!" I'm told He took a week's vacation to recuperate.

What about Doug? Well, he was an even tougher nut to crack. God immediately began working on his spiritual re-birth too, but Doug's spiritual "pregnancy" had already lasted 25 years with no spiritual birth in sight when God made another desperate move–made Doug a cop on midnights and pulled strings to get me hired as a part-time secretary in the "Cop Shop." Like they say, "God works in MYSTERIOUS ways."

When I went to work at the Police Department and met Doug, I figured him for a totally lost cause. Nice guy and nice to talk to, but HOPELESSLY wild. He lived what the Chinese call "an interesting life." But it was even–he considered me a HOPELESS stick in the mud. But God can meet any challenge, so He had Doug transferred from midnights to days where he was FORCED to be around me.

*Well, my tongue flapped just as much in those days as in these and one day I told him that some foreign missionaries were going to be staying at my home for a few days. "Pfft!" Doug sputtered. "**Mercenaries**, you mean! They live off what they beg of other people's money!" From that auspicious beginning came three years of my explaining biblical principles and his listening and asking questions. He was different from me in that he KNEW he wasn't a Christian and had no doubt about where he was heading when he died and...let's just say he wasn't looking forward to the trip.*

FINALLY, after three years of yammering with him, he came to me one day and said, "You know, I don't know why He'd do it for someone like me, but I know Christ died for me." He was 28 human years old, but was a brand new "spiritual baby." A few years ago he told me he had been out walking in a field and thinking about the Bible verses I'd shown him when, "...all of a sudden everything just fell into place and I KNEW it was right." That was the moment his spiritual pregnancy was over and God sealed in the "Spirit Section" that had been missing.

"...having believed *(that Christ died and rose again to pay the penalty for your sins)* **you were SEALED with the Holy Spirit of promise, who is the guarantee of our inheritance..." Eph. 1:13-14**

And now you know the truth that you've probably always surmised...Doug was "born" in a field somewhere and maybe that's why he's a little strange now! Anyway...I'm told God needed a MONTH's vacation to recuperate from Doug's pregnancy! And you know what? Now Doug gives some of HIS money to missionaries so they can help other people get through their spiritual "pregnancies." What a difference a birth makes!

"As many as received Christ, to them He gave the right to be the children of God—to those who believe in His name; who were BORN, not of the will of the flesh...but of God." John 1:12, 13.
Explanation: ** *Several months earlier Doug had fallen off the roof of our house and landed with very little ceremony—but a lot of bounce—on a three inch high stump of a small tree. Fortunately, he lived through it, but he'll never live it down.*

The Terrible Parable of 50 Years From Now This Won't Matter!

Diary Entry - 1968: My two-year old was climbing all over me. "Why don't you go play with the other kids, Bryan?" I suggested wistfully. But being the youngest of three children has its frustrations and, burying his head in my lap, he wailed pitifully, "But, MOMMY!! I will be the rotten EGG in the race!"

I could have told my blond-headed moppet, "Honey, fifty years from now this won't matter," and I'd have been right… because within fifty <u>minutes</u> his frustration was past and he forgot he was the rotten-egg runner. But the other day I was frustrated. The shoe was on the other foot and it pinched!

It was day two of one of my three-day migraine headaches; our dog, despite a tomato juice bath, still smelled a WHOLE lot like skunk and, as we started out, an on-coming Kamikaze tourist—driving with both eyes on the lake instead of at least one eye on the road—used OUR side of the double yellow lines at the same time as we were passing a jogger! "The whole WORLD is out to get me today!" I shrieked, cringing in the passenger's seat as we braked, swerved, and missed both jogger and Kamikaze tourist. I could feel myself crawling further up the walls of irritation, frustration and self-pity to a near disaster level. Then I remembered—"Fifty Years From Now This Won't Matter"—and I was back in control.

*Now! All those who know me are saying—in voices **dripping** with sarcasm, "NOTHING will matter for that old girl in fifty years!! She'll be six feet under and pushing up daisies!" In one way they're right—all the frustrations of this life—family problems, money problems, health problems—will be past and won't matter. But, in another way, they're wrong! Oh, I'll be flower fertilizer all right, but how I live my life before a little man in his black suit slams the lid down on my casket WILL matter in fifty years. To Whom? To ME!! Because I'm a Christian.*

All the frustrations of YOUR life will be over in 50 or so years too unless you are still DISGUSTINGLY young! Are you a Christian through faith in Christ as your personal Lord and Savior? If you are, the Bible teaches that the Lord has reserved a spot for you in heaven, but neither your faith nor mine will allow either of us to sidestep the Judgment Seat of Christ where every Christian's life's works AFTER they become a Christian will be put through a testing of fire. Sorry 'bout that, but…

*"**…we must ALL** (referring to Christians) **appear before the judgment seat of Christ, that each one may receive** (rewards for) **the things done while they were in the** (physical) **body … whether good or bad.**" II Corin. 5:10.*

*"**…each one's work will become clear…because it will be revealed by <u>fire</u>; and the fire will test each one's work, of what sort it is.**" I Corin. 3:13.*

*The PURPOSE of this testing is to allow God to hand out rewards to His faithful children—sort of like a human father would hand out an inheritance to his offspring… "**If anyone's work which he has built on it** ("it" being the foundation of faith in Christ. vs. 11) **survives the fire, he will receive a <u>reward.</u>**" **I Corin. 3:14.** Since the testing of my life's actions is for the purpose of rewards, why am I cringing? Aren't I a nice person? Well, sort of, but I KNOW me! I've got this nice veneer that I've trained to hide my real feelings in certain situations. God's going to look PAST that veneer and check out my HEART! "**Judge*** *nothing before the Lord comes, who will bring to light the hidden things of darkness and reveal the counsels of the <u>hearts.</u>" (I Corin. 4:5).*

Any sweet words I've spoken or good deeds I've done that merely looked good or sounded good to others but weren't performed with a willing heart and a right attitude will burn as **"wood, hay or stubble"** *(I* **Corin. 3:12)** *in a HUGE blaze and end up as an embarrassing pile of ashes at the Lord's feet! Conversely, however, I've probably innocently said or done things for which I've been roundly and erroneously condemned by my fellow man. The Lord will check out the motives of my heart and vindicate me on those.*

Let's not even TALK about the ornery things I've done on purpose. We KNOW those will be clinkers! I'm gonna have a mile-high pile of ashes, but there'll be a few "works" in that mess that'll come out as sparkling **"gold, silver and precious stones." (I Corin. 3:12)** *The Lord is so gracious to His children. He assures us that if EVERYTHING a believer does after salvation ends up as ashes, He'll still not drop kick that "child" past the goal posts of heaven into hell...***"If anyone's work is burned, he will suffer loss** *(of rewards)* **but he himself will be saved..."** *I Corin. 3:15. Comforting, huh?*

The Bible isn't very specific as to what good these rewards are gonna do for you or for me after we have 'em. And you know, it really doesn't matter to me anymore. When I was first saved and became one of God's children, I was an extremely mercenary soul and the idea of getting rewards made my greedy little eyes WIDE and SPARKLEY with anticipation! But the Lord has a way of changing one's values. You know how hard you try to please a close friend, a parent or spouse because you CARE about them and they care about you? MOST of the time I want to please God because He cares so much about me.

So now I live a PERFECT life, right? Har-R-R-R-R!!! I said "MOST" of the time. Where's that Kamikaze tourist? If I get a whack at him, I might scream unkind comments about his driving while kicking him in the shins! It wouldn't fill his day with sunshine, but—as he hopped around on one leg trying to dodge this insane Vermonter—I'd be able to console him by screeching...

.............***IN FIFTY YEARS, THIS WON'T MATTER, you <u>CRUM!!</u>***

...OR WILL IT? Hmmmm....Guess it WILL! Have YOU accepted Christ as your Savior? If you have, we'll both have bonfires in the Lord's presence. I'll invite you to my bonfire if you'll invite me to yours and after our ashes cool I hope we find a whole BUNCH of jewels in my life's ashes and in yours.

The Terrible Parable of the Best Christmas

"For unto us a child is born...unto us a Son is given; and the government shall be upon His shoulder; and His name shall be called Wonderful, Counselor, The Mighty God, The Everlasting Father, the Prince of Peace." Isa. 9:6.

It was Christmas 50+ years ago. Hadn't slept most of the night. Felt uncomfortable and miserable. Then sharp pains forced me to be admitted to the hospital and I had to miss going to my mother-in-law's house for Christmas dinner and she was an EXCELLENT cook! Found out later that, in the hustle and bustle, some of the late-arriving members of the family (that got to EAT Christmas dinner) didn't even MISS me until sometime in the afternoon when someone finally asked, "Where's Carolyn?" It was about the best Christmas I've ever had!

Maybe I should explain. On December 25, 1962, at 9:30 a.m., unto me a child was born. My very own son. His needs "governed" how my household was run, and I called him Wonderful!

I remember feeling particularly blessed that Jeff had been born on the day we celebrate Christ's birthday. Brought him home from the hospital and put Christmas wrapping paper around him, laid him under the Christmas tree and took a picture of my precious "Christmas gift."

Jeff didn't share my outlook about his birthday. He complained loud and long that he never got to have a "real" birthday party. None of his friends could come on Christmas Day and he'd wail... "REAL birthday parties are held on your real birth DAY, Mom!" We tried to give him a "half-birthday party" in July, but he'd have none of it! If the government had been upon JEFF'S shoulder, he'd have issued a decree changing Christmas to the end of June!

"Unto us a child is born..." I wonder if Mary felt blessed that first Christmas. Every child born on this earth is a blessing...a unique, one-of-a-kind miracle. When Mary looked down at Jesus that very first time, did she perhaps see that He had her eyes, her olive skin and maybe her Uncle Joe Bob's chin? After all, He was human and He carried Mary's genes.

"Unto us a Son is given." But Jesus was also God who had existed from eternity past. Therefore, as the eternal Son of God, He could not be "born" but simply "given." Even though the Bible teaches that no man has seen God at any time, do you suppose Mary wondered if His tiny hands looked like His Father's hands or if He had His Father's nose?

I looked at Jeff and saw a beautiful, healthy baby boy, but I had no clue as to what lay ahead for him. If I could have seen his future, would I have cringed at the hard times ahead and rejoiced for all the good times he'd have?

Did Mary know what lay ahead for her new son? Did she know the prophesy of Isaiah 9:6? "...the government shall be upon His shoulder: His name shall be called Wonderful, Counselor, The Mighty God, The Everlasting Father, The Prince of Peace." If she knew these things, did she wonder how such tiny shoulders could ever carry the responsibilities of the government upon them? Did it seem real to her that this tiny child truly was The Mighty God...The Prince of Peace? I wonder.

We, as parents, rejoice when our children do well and we all hurt FOR our children when they suffer any harm. I wonder...did Mary know ALL the prophesies concerning the Savior she had been chosen to raise? The prophesies in the Isaiah 9:6 passage would have made her heart soar! But what about some of these: Psalm 22:16 "His hands and feet were to be pierced;" Psalm 41:9 "He would be betrayed by a friend;" Psalm 69:20, 21 ***"He would be given vinegar and gall to drink;"*** *and Psalm 22:18–**"People would cast lots for His clothing**." How would I have felt if those things were prophesied for MY son? And those are some of the gentler prophesies about Jesus' death on the cross that purchased Mary's salvation, your salvation and mine.*

Those prophesies were all literally fulfilled while Mary could only watch and hurt FOR Jesus on the sidelines. (God couldn't use Mary's help in providing salvation. Mary needed a Savior herself and she knew it! In Luke 1:47 Mary says, ***"My spirit rejoiced in God my <u>Savior</u>."***) *Did she think of these things that first Christmas...or did she put them out of her mind while she held that tiny hand that would one day be pierced for her, for you, and for me?*

*This Christmas, as you are gathered with your own children, take a moment to think back to that first Christmas...and thank Him for being willing to come as Mary's tiny child...knowing that He was coming to die. And think whether YOU would have wanted to be chosen for Mary's job that first Christmas...**The Best Christmas!***

Jeff - Then and Now

The Terrible Parable of_____'s Wonderfulness

(**DIRECTIONS**: *This is a test...this is ONLY a test. Do not pass "Go" and do NOT collect $200.00. But DO write YOUR name in each of the blanks of this Parable to see how you do.*)

Bryan was barely 2 years old and my diary has this telling entry:

April 1, 1968 - **Bryan's language is improving rapidly. So is his cunning. Now whenever something goes amiss, he always tells me, "Jeffy did it" or "Kenny did it." Never once does he EVER put any blame on "Bryan."**

I doubt there is anyone who would judge a two-year old very harshly for claiming innocence of all evil deeds, but it always amuses me when I come across a grown adult who claims to be pure as the driven snow. Do you feel your record is definitely better than the <u>average</u> and that the Lord will be thrilled to usher you past those pearly gates of heaven? If you do, this is directed to YOU! Even if you KNOW you're not as good as you should be, this is directed to you ANYWAY!

Hey, _____!!

I've been THINKING about you! Oh ye who hasn't hurt many people and who is as good as most people and better than others and who, therefore, feels confident that heaven's gates will be opened to grant you entrance thereto. This is directed to YOU!!

You have such an innocent, angelic little face but, you know, I have noted no halo floating above your head. Now, you can tell me you're PERFECT and deserve such a halo but, if you do, I'm sure you won't mind if I check with your FAMILY to see if this missing halo is an oversight on the Lord's part or if it's missing for SEVERAL very good reasons. 1 MAY even be forced to remind you of your well-hidden, securely-locked closet hiding the skeletons of actions performed by you or words spoken by you that you wish you could undo or retract.

You DO have that closet, DON'T you!? I knew it. 'Cause I have one, too!

Okay. You will agree that you're not a TOTALLY perfect human being, right? But COMPARED TO OTHER HUMANS, you're pretty good! Brings to mind a verse which proves your point!

"For all OTHER humans have sinned <u>WORSE</u>, and come short of _____'s glory." Romans 3:23

Oh! Wait! Wait! I slightly misquoted that verse. Seems it should be:

"...for <u>ALL</u> humans have sinned and come short of the glory of <u>GOD!</u>" Romans 3:23.

Oh, dear! If the Bible is true, there goes your theory. It seems God won't compare you to other HUMANS when he passes out either judgment or eternal life. He'll compare you to HIMSELF and here is how you'll stack up:

"But we ALL (including _____) **are like an unclean thing, and all our righteousnesses** (good things we've done) **are as FILTHY RAGS." Isaiah 64:6**

_____'s heart is deceitful above ALL things and desperately wicked. Who can know it?" Jeremiah 17:9

"There is NO human that does good, no, NOT ONE (including _____). **Their throat is an open tomb." Romans 3:13**

8

NOW! If I'm reading this correctly, your goodnesses (and my wonderfulness) in comparison to God's goodness comes out as filthy rags or a gaping hole with decaying matter inside. How many filthy rags and open graves do you suppose will be welcome in heaven?

You have several options at this point:

1. *Hope the Bible is wrong on this aspect, even though the Bible has been 100% accurate so far!*
2. *Start working on an asbestos suit that will withstand high temperatures;*
3. *Hope like crazy that I'm crazy; OR–*
4. *Accept God's free gift of salvation which confers God's righteousness on us grungy humans ...*

"...to _____who does not work (for salvation) **but *believes* on him (Christ) who justifies the ungodly, _____'s FAITH is accounted for RIGHTEOUSNESS."** *Romans 4:5*

"...if_____ shall confess with his mouth (that Christ died for his sins) **and shall believe in his heart that God raised Christ from the dead, _____ shall be saved. For with the heart _____ believes unto righteousness and with his mouth confession is made unto salvation. Romans 10:9,10.**

If you have God's righteousness instead of your own faulty righteousness," you're slid past those pearly gates...

"He who believes in the Son *has* everlasting life..."

But–REJECT Christ's offer to pay the penalty for your misdeeds (SINS!! we're talking here!) and God's free gift of righteousness and you get...

(DIRECTION: *Put your name in this next blank* ONLY if you don't believe that Christ died to pay for your sins and rose again. Otherwise, put in "whosoever")*

*"... and * _____ does **NOT** believe the Son shall not see life, but the WRATH of God abides on him." John 3:36.*

Take your pick, _____! I've chosen Christ. I've always hated trying to sew asbestos!

The Terrible Parable of the Christmas Photograph

Diary Entry - 12/20/69. Bryan was holding a Christmas card that featured a photo of the manger scene and was inspired to recite his piece for the Christmas Eve service: "Little Jesus is His name. High from heaven, down He came." Then he carefully jabbed a pudgy finger directly on the manger and ad libbed, "... and He landed _right_ _there_!"

Brings visions of a carefully-aimed baby cannon-balling out of the heavens and crashing right into that manger, doesn't it? Well, Christ WAS in heaven before He was incarnated here on earth, so the kid had his theology right! What more can you ask from an almost-four-year-old? I'm not sure how long he held that slightly offbeat impression of Christ's birth. I know I held some half-baked impressions of the Christmas story for quite some time myself. Take the bit about the way Mary and Joseph dressed this baby...

...in a make-shift suit of swaddling cloth! You'd have thought Mary would have had enough sense to bring along the baby clothes she had undoubtedly been making for nine months. SURELY she knew that this trip was close to her due date!! How could she have been so unprepared? _I'd_ have packed baby clothes!

And the wise men...if they were so wise, why didn't they bring decent gifts for a young child? The gold I could understand–start His bank account early–compounded interest counts up quickly–the child can retire early–GOOD move! But they also carried spices and tree sap around with them for nearly two years while they wandered around looking for this Child! Tree sap? Yes, tree sap! Frankincense is tree sap! They bowed down, worshiped Him, and gave Him tree sap and spices! Hardly appropriate gifts for a toddler. I've bought people strange gifts in my time, but TREE SAP for a little Boy!? Didn't they read Dr. Spock in those days? Leggo's–jumbo sized. That's what I'd have brought Him. Something appropriate!

Sticking with the wise men...King Herod, in an attempt to eliminate any usurper to his throne, destroyed all the babies two years old and under after he realized the wise men were wise enough not to tell him where this King of the Jews could be found. Which means it took at LEAST a year and a half for these wise men to get to King Herod to ask where to FIND Jesus in the first place. What TOOK them so long? They forget to pack the road maps? Their camels go on a sit-down strike? They waited for the tree sap to run in the spring?...WHAT!? They knew the Child was born "King of the Jews," so if they were THAT smart, couldn't they just head west and hit Israel in a couple months? P-f-f-t! They needed a wise **_woman's_** guiding hand to plan this trip, that's all!

I always liked one part though...the bit about the shepherds getting the news first from the angelic hosts. It _meant_ nothing to me, but I liked it. There they sat...in the dark...minding their sheep like every other night when they got the beejeebers scared out of them by a whole passel of angels singing at the top of their lungs (Do angels have lungs?). What an _experience_ to reminisce about and retell over and over to the grandkids!

The birth of Jesus was a fantastic event–but I felt the individual aspects of the story made about as much sense as Bryan's cannon-balling-baby bit. Or had I just been looking at it wrong?

I think of the Bible as God's photo album in written form. It contains hundreds of fuzzy photos that He develops and brings into focus bit by bit as we allow Him to adjust the camera lenses of our minds. I think He's been fiddling with the adjustment button on my "camera lens" cause....

... The picture of the baby clothes? It seems swaddling cloth was the material in which the dead were wrapped for burial back then. Jesus came to earth—not primarily to live, but primarily to die. He was wrapped in the picture He was to fully develop and put in complete focus some thirty-odd years later on the cross...which made swaddling cloth the <u>perfect</u> material to wrap that Baby in.

The ridiculous toddler gifts? The wise men came to worship the King spoken of in Jewish scriptures. They must have been wise enough to read about the Jewish tabernacle because they figured out that gold speaks of deity; they recognized this tiny Child to be God incarnate and brought the appropriate symbol to prove it! And the tree sap and spice? Frankincense was mixed with spices and burned on the altar of incense in the tabernacle whenever prayer was lifted up to God. So, I admit it... they brought PERFECT gifts that acknowledged Jesus as God to whom their prayers should be offered.

*The shepherds being honored with the news of Jesus' birth first? For thousands of years shepherds had assisted God by lovingly raising the fuzzy photo He had used of the coming Savior—innocent lambs which were sacrificed in the temple. Seems fair to me that God should honor the shepherds by letting them be the first to know that the innocent "Lamb" He dearly loved was now in the world. John said of Jesus, **"Behold the LAMB of God."** (And it is believed that these were the temple shepherds that received the news!)*

Go back to those wise men for a minute. They wandered around nearly two years before they found someone who understood the scriptures and pointed them towards Christ. All those who have found Christ as Savior down through the centuries have wandered through life until people tell them enough about Christ for them to finally "get the picture in focus" and then take God at His word. The problem is, the older and wiser people are about the ways of this world, the harder it is for them to believe God when He says salvation is free to all takers.

The Bible says we must come to Christ "as a child" would. Offer a small child the gift of a lollipop that costs five cents, five bucks or five HUNDRED bucks and the reaction is the same—<u>everything</u> on the kid wiggles, a grin breaks out as he makes a grab for it, and there is absolutely NO thought of repaying you for your gift. Try to give an adult <u>anything</u>, especially something costly—salvation was VERY costly to Christ—and their eyes narrow, they pull back and say with great suspicion, "What's the catch?"

Since it took me half of forever to understand that Christ loved me enough to be born to die, I'd like to think I'm an <u>extremely</u> wise person. But I don't think I'll ask, because I'm afraid God would look at me with great love, shake His head, and just smile knowingly. I'd <u>HATE</u> that.

Ah-h-h-h well. Merry Christmas all!! Enjoy!!

The Terrible Parable of the Change of Fur

__Diary Entry: November 24, 1972__ – The kids were playing "Horsie & Doggie"—a strange game where one child was the "Master" and the other two crawled around on all fours as the "horse" and "dog." Jeff, who was the "horse" that day, was wearing B.P. pants (Before Patches) so to prevent his ventilating the knees, I interrupted a chase scene with: "If you're playing that, you'll have to change out of your good school pants!" Cooperative horse that he was, Jeff whinnied in a high horsie voice, "Okay. Me go change my fur."

So! I raised kids who had a few quirks. They came by it honestly. I have vivid memories of myself at age 5 or so climbing into the back of my dad's farm truck and singing "opera" at the top of my lungs for an audience consisting entirely of the barnyard chickens who had NO appreciation of my talents, merely cocked their heads at the "high C's" in my repertoire, and totally ignored my costume changes. But mom noticed and…not understanding that she was speaking to the star of the "Met"…forced me to stop changing clothes between every "number."

Yeah, I was off-beat from way back then, but I considered God to be more so. God did things that made sense to NO ONE as far as I could tell. Take the account of Jesus' grand entrance into Jerusalem on Palm Sunday riding on a donkey. From the time I was a small child I remember questioning the appropriateness of Jesus' mode of transportation. What kind of grand entrance was that? – riding on a DONKEY! There He was…proclaiming that He was king of the Jewish people, and the best He could come up with was a DONKEY?!!

Just who was responsible for hiring this guy's P.R. man anyway? I'd have had Him come in riding a magnificent white stallion that would have pranced down that dusty little road tossing it's regal head and stepping high! Now THAT would have been an entrance befitting a KING!

I continued in my contempt-filled ignorance on this subject until a few years back. I was browsing through McGee's __Thru the Bible__ series and he happened to mention that Oriental kings ALWAYS rode donkeys in peace time. The only time they rode a charging white (or any other color) stallion was when they were going into battle. OH!! Suddenly Christ's choice of transport for His grand entrance was no longer something to hold in contempt. Instead, it was PERFECT!!

Christ came the first time as the peaceful, docile "Lamb of God"…offering Himself as the sacrifice for man's sin, Savior of the world, and King to the Jewish nation if they would choose to accept Him. Of COURSE he would ride the donkey. That's what oriental kings RODE when they came in peace.

Here, all these years I had been wishing Christ had "changed the donkey's fur" to that of a stallion when that would have pictured Him as a warrior…totally the wrong image for His first advent. Okay, Lord, you knew best all these years and I was wrong….again!!

HOWEVER!! My idea of what constitutes a grand entrance WILL be utilized some day. Fortunately, it's at least 7 years away…and depending on how long this age of grace lasts, possibly many, many years away.

For nearly 2,000 years now Christ has been the patient, gentle God who treats us in grace while He allows mankind free will to choose either for or against Him. But this age won't last forever. And at the end of the seven years of the Tribulation (which will come into this world after this Age of Grace is completed), unbelievers will see a drastic "change of fur." Revelation 19:11 warns the world:

"Now I saw heaven opened and behold a white HORSE and He who sat on it was called Faithful and True, and in righteousness He JUDGES and MAKES WAR. And His name is called "The Word of God."

*Ah HA!!! NEXT time He comes, He'll use the warrior's horse. How do we know this is Christ on the horse? In John 1:14 it says of Christ **"…the Word became flesh."***

Revelation paints the word picture of Christ coming to earth as a warrior on a rearing, head-tossing, high-stepping white stallion. He won't be coming as the gentle Savior of mankind. He'll be coming as mankind's "Judge," and to "make war" on those who have rejected Him, which totally harmonizes with the rest of scripture's teaching.

What an amazingly accurate picture God gave of Christ's two advents with just a "change of fur."

There are countless word pictures used in the Bible. It's my personal opinion…totally unsubstantiated by scripture, so don't panic yet…that all who get to heaven will be required to understand the pictures God painted for us in His Word before we're allowed to graduate to the bigger and better things He has planned. Since it took me nearly 50 years to understand one tiny spiritual picture, I certainly hope my rate of understanding improves when I get my resurrection body or I'll be enrolled in "Spiritual Pictures 101" half of forever!

It may not be too bad, though. At least God never used the picture of a slightly off-beat child climbing into a farm truck and singing opera to a bunch of chickens. The good Lord could make a sensible picture out of that if He wanted to since He's all powerful, but I doubt He'd WANT to!!

The Terrible Parable of a Chip-Off-the-Old-Block

Diary Entry - September 18, 1968 – _I was making chocolate chip cookies and had two pans of cookies ready to put in the oven. I had to leave for a minute and when I came back I found that one cookie had mysteriously disappeared. I knew I had found my culprit when Bryan (age 2 1/2) came back into the kitchen with VERY sticky fingers, grinned at me and said, "That was duhd!" (How do I SPELL that to rhyme with "good?")_

The kid was a chip off the old block....had inherited his mom's sweet tooth! I STILL love chocolate chip cookie dough. And since Bryan was also a chubby, tow-headed CHARMER at that age, culprit or not, I probably just smiled and gave him another spoonful of cookie dough. I had very few defenses against some of his tactics!

It seems to be the ability of all small children to develop tactics which outwit adults, allowing them to obtain the desires of their little hearts. I've been told that I was the imp of the family when I was small too, so perhaps I shouldn't have been surprised at Bryan's ingenuity in getting his own way. When he was a little older and allowed to go to a few houses down the block, he was SUPPOSED to knock on the door and wait to be invited in. Instead, he'd march straight in, flash a huge smile and announce to surprised adults, "My Mommy SAID I could come in." NONE of the neighbors would make him go back out and knock first—despite repeated requests from me not to tolerate his monkeyshines.

That was 50 years ago and I THINK he knocks now before going into someone else's home. He got married a while back and I know he and his wife want to have children. I can hardly WAIT to see if their offspring will be chips-off-Bryan's-old-block and will act just like him!

God PLANNED all this chip-off-the-old-block stuff, you know. He uses human traits to explain spiritual relationships which He has founded, not on an "old block," but on "The Rock."

Christ is referred to as "the Rock" in many places in the Bible: **"God is the _rock_ of my salvation; I will say unto _God_ my _rock_; They drank of that spiritual _rock_ and that _Rock_ was Christ..."** to quote a few.

In Matthew 16 there is a wonderful play on words that becomes evident in the original Greek. Jesus tells Peter, **"You are Peter** (pet_ros_—meaning "a stone") **and upon this Rock** (pet_ra_—meaning "a massive rock," referring to Himself) **I will build my church"** (or household of believers).

Peter acted so much like Jesus that Jesus called him "a-stone-off-the-Old-Massive-Rock" and gave Peter the position of a foundation "stone" for the church. Eph. 2:20 says that believers are _members_ of the household of God, having been built on the foundation of the apostles and prophets..."

Peter, the other apostles, and the Old Testament prophets all acted like "stones-off-the-Old-Massive Rock" so God could use their witness to start His "building program." But Christ Himself had to come to earth to be the Massive Rock needed for the cornerstone: **"Christ _Himself_ being the chief cornerstone." Eph.2:20.** No mere mortal could bear the weight of His spiritual church.

Well, if Christ is the "Massive Rock" forming the cornerstone of the church and the apostles and prophets are foundation "stones," what positions are left for all us Johnny-come-lately Christians of today? I guess we must be building "pebbles." A chip off a rock is a 'pebble," right? Bryan was just a little guy when he *believed that Christ died and rose again to provide him salvation. Immediately, he became a "pebble-off-the-Old-Massive-Rock"—a tiny (but charming) building block God sealed with the mortar of the Holy Spirit which guarantees Bryan will receive his inheritance as a child of God.*

"You trusted in Christ <u>after</u> you heard the gospel and, <u>having believed</u>, you were <u>sealed</u> with the Holy Spirit...who is the <u>guarantee</u> of our inheritance..." Eph. 1:13, 14.

For the last 2,000 years the Lord has been sealing hordes of "pebbles" into His church—one at a time—as individuals come to trust Christ as their Savior.

But even though we "pebbles" are sealed with the permanent mortar of the Holy Spirit, we're still free to wiggle in any direction we choose. We can wiggle totally like unbelievers, only worry about things of this life, and stack up treasures on this earth—which may last for 100 years IF we were smart enough to choose parents with longevity in their genes.

OR *we can wiggle in God's direction at least SOME of the time and act like "pebbles-off-the-Old-Massive-Rock" and stack up treasures that will **ADD TO** our inheritance in heaven for eternity—which will last CONSIDERABLY longer than 100 years.*

We "pebbles" can wiggle in many ways pleasing to God, but if you want a REALLY interesting and rewarding life, you can wage war against Satan himself. No joke? No joke!!

*Christ said, **"I will build my church, and the gates of Hell will not prevail against It."**...**Matthew 16:18**. I had skimmed right over that verse oodles of times, always assuming that Satan and his forces were the attackers and Christ's church (along with me in it) was cringing in a corner somewhere. But look at the picture painted here. In Biblical times, cities were walled as protection against their enemies.*

*If an attack was imminent, the leaders slammed those gates shut and all the people within those walls were unreachable—as long as the gates held up under the attack. The "gates of Hell" belong to Satan—not to Christ. So the picture we have here is that, when we "pebbles" <u>act</u> like the Old Massive Rock and go on the offense, Satan's defenses crumble and people can slip through the cracks in that gate—**IF** they want to—and can become one of Christ's "pebbles."*

What ammunition do we use? The simple Gospel.

"For I am not ashamed of the Gospel of Christ, for <u>it is the power of God</u> to salvation for everyone who <u>believes</u>... Romans 1:16. *Believes what? That Christ died for me—shed His blood to pay the price God demanded in payment for my sin, was buried, arose from the dead, and will come again to take me home to be with Him in glory when my life on this earth is done.*

My chip-off-the-old-block would walk into neighbors' homes and cheerily announce, "My Mommy SAID I could come in!" He didn't know it then, but he was doing EXACTLY what God says we can do as "pebbles-off-the-Old-Massive-Rock." We can walk right up to the enemy's gate, cheerily announce, "My Heavenly Father SAID I should come in!"...and explain the good news of the Gospel until someone understands, believes it, and slips through the crack we put in Satan's gate. Can't you just SEE Satan stomping around as he loses another soul to Christ? Don't you just LOVE IT?!

Are you one of God's "pebbles" through faith in Christ? If you are, GREAT!! Let's go put another crack in Satan's gate!

The Terrible Parable of Dad's Family Plan

Instructions: *Put a baby or child's name in the blanks marked ("B") (or put your OWN name in there) and the father's name in the blanks marked ("F").*

Well _____(B), how do you like being _____'s (F) child so far? Let's see. So far you were planted as a seed in an "apartment" where you had to grow for nine months in an INCREDIBLY cramped position. Then you were evicted without reasonable notice into a bigger apartment, which was an improvement, but one where you had to be wrapped in layers and layers of scratchy material just to keep you warm. You could barely WIGGLE!

Before you were moved into the bigger apartment you NEVER felt hungry and never had to beg for food. NOW you have to ask for food every time you want some and sometimes dad is so incredibly slow in providing for you that you end up crying! I know your dad is trying hard, but I've heard that sometimes you feel tired and cranky and dad just can't seem to fix what's wrong. Sometimes he even lets you fuss and fuss without seeming to CARE! In some ways it was easier and nicer before you were evicted out of your first tiny apartment!

I've also heard that your dad forced you to go into a little chamber of horrors and actually PAID to have a horrible little man in a white jacket poke holes in your tender little body and inject stuff that made you feel just AWFUL! I've heard that you are keeping up a brave front and smile at this horrible father whenever you can, but it's HARD, isn't it?

Well, _____(B), I hate to break the news to you, but it's going to get WORSE! And your father is to blame! Don't let on that I told you, but he's going to expect you to learn to walk and get around on your own two feet without being carried. Yes, it's TRUE! And what's more, he's going to force you to learn to <u>speak</u>—in SENTENCES, no less. And you'll have to say "please" and "thank you" EVERY TIME you want something or he gives you anything. Can you believe it?

And the man is NEVER going to be satisfied. No matter how much you learn, he's going to want more, More, MORE out of you! Did you know before you started in on this life stuff that your very own father was going to force you to go to school 180 days of EVERY year for at LEAST 12 years!!!?? He'll tell you all these things are for your own good, but you're going to doubt that statement a good many times.

You'd think learning all this stuff would be enough, wouldn't you? But NO!!! He's going to make a SLAVE out of you. You'll be expected to make your bed and wash dishes and probably even clean your room and MOW THE LAWN!

And since you have to learn all these things from scratch, you're going to make mistakes. He'll go real easy on you at first, but after you're older, he's gonna expect you to do things RIGHT! And he's gonna expect you to do what you know to be right without being REMINDED you have to do them. And if you get on your high horse and back talk to him—WATCH OUT!!! You'll get your little tail feathers in all KINDS of trouble.

When you're a teenager, he's going to want you to hang out with the right crowd and act responsibly. Gee, do you want to reconsider going through this whole "Life with Father" routine now before its too late? What's that? Oh, yes, I guess it is ALREADY too late since you've been born into his family, isn't it?

What? You'd like to know if there's a benefit package involved here...to sort of off-set the down side, huh? Well, let's see. There COULD be a good side to this story. Dad DOES love you an awfully lot. _____(B), do you know that he told me you were incredibly special and that you and the other kids in his family are the most important things in the world to him? It IS nice to be loved, I guess.

And if you learn all the things he's going to try to teach you, you will be a productive person in this society and in your dad's family, which will please him immensely and will benefit you, too, in the long run. He'd like you to grow up to have high standards and high morals. I guess that's not a BAD way to be, is it?

If you remember, he's given you wonderful gifts. The gift of life is the most precious one he could give, but you also have more toys than any one child needs, don't you? What's more, he's never let you starve, has he? You aren't always fed just when you want, perhaps, but those little cheeks sure prove you're well cared for. And when you need help learning to tie your shoes, you know dad will be there for you. Or, when you need ten bucks for an ice cream cone (I'm taking inflation into account here, dad) you know you'll be able to ask dad for it. Sometimes he may say "no" because it wouldn't be the right time for it, but sometimes you'll get that ice cream too.

And after your dad has taught you all he knows and gets incredibly old and "passes on," he'll leave you all the wealth he has accumulated during this lifetime as another proof that he loves you. You know, _____(B) maybe being _____(F)'s child isn't too bad a deal after all.

You know where I'm heading with all this, don't you!? Life in God's family follows the same path as a child in YOUR family. The Bible says the Word of God is the "seed" that grows into faith, and faith in Christ's death, burial and resurrection is what allows you to be a child in God's family– **"As many as receive Christ, to them God gives the right to become CHILDREN of GOD, to those who BELIEVE in Christ's name...who are BORN...of God."** *John 1:12, 13.*

As you grow from a newborn "spiritual baby" in Christ's family and through spiritual childhood into spiritual maturity, you may have to learn a lot of new things, survive some hard things, and have some pain. If you rebel and get too far out of line, you'll probably get your tail feathers paddled. And sometimes you fuss and fuss over a problem and God doesn't even seem to CARE–at least He doesn't seem to care on a timely basis.

Just because you are born into God's family by faith in Christ doesn't mean life will always be easy. You may not get everything you want or get it when you want it, but He'll do what's best for you. And you'll know that whatever He brings into your life is for the purpose of keeping you in line, helping you grow spiritually, or to trust Him more and become more like Him.

And you'll know that He loves you totally because you're His own dear child, born into His family by faith. He gives the gifts of ETERNAL life after this one, inner peace and assurance in this life and sends His Spirit to live within you to teach you spiritual truth.

Besides, He has a TERRIFIC fringe benefits package! Where else are you going to get justified and glorified for pity sakes! **"We know that ALL THINGS work together for good to those who love God, to those who are the called according to His purpose. For whom He foreknew, He also predestined to be conformed to the image of His son. Moreover, whom He predestined, them He also called; whom He called He also justified; and whom He justified, these He also glorified!"** **Romans 8:28-30**

Some people feel that being a Christian isn't worth much, but I guess it depends on how you look at it, doesn't it?

Dad's Trip Home

I flew in from Vermont to Ohio to be with Dad and was horrified as I came into his hospital room and heard him call towards heaven, "LORD, FORGIVE ME FOR MY SINS!! Have MERCY on me!!"… not once, but several times.

Dad had always been the strong, silent type. He didn't take kindly to others trying to force their ways or opinions on him and, by George, he wasn't going to inflict his ways or opinions on anyone else either. He NEVER talked about religion, except he would refer to Christ's return with utter confidence, head nodding and arthritic finger pointing toward the recipient of his wisdom, "He's coming back by about the year 2000. Yes, sir! I believe it's gonna be pretty close to then."

Dad was 82 before I heard an actual confession of faith from his lips. In the course of a conversation when I was comforting Mom about a grandchild who had been killed in a car accident the year before, I slipped in, "Dad, what did Christ do for you?" and wondered with what response, if any, he'd favor me. To my utter amazement, he stuck that arthritic finger close to my face and declared with great feeling, "He D-I-I-E-D for me!" and my heart soared. It was two years later when he contracted the ALS (Lou Gehrig's Disease) that landed him in that hospital where he was crying out for forgiveness.

As I listened, I realized that Dad had never grasped the doctrine of eternal security of the believer and, when we were alone, I gently started to tell him some scripture verses and explain them. Well, that wasn't quite right. "I KNOW all that!" He not-so-gently exploded. So I tried a different tact. I found that he was now willing to talk about spiritual things, so I brought up the subject often and let him go with it where he would. I found he had a good knowledge of many spiritual truths.

Finally, during one weekend visit I asked him, "Dad, am I ever going to be Aunt Nellie's child?" He looked at me as though I had lost every last marble he had worked so hard to pound into my head. "No," he answered and waited for his youngest daughter go on with this strange conversation.

"I was born into your family, wasn't I? Through all eternity, I'll be Gerald Humphrey's daughter. I can't ever get into Aunt Nellie's family because I wasn't BORN to her, right? Still confused, but interested, he agreed. "Did I ever do anything you didn't like? Anything that made you angry?" "NAH!" he said emphatically. "I moved to Vermont!" I reminded him. (And chose not to remind him of anything further than that) "W-e-e-l-l-l…." he conceded. (He hadn't been thrilled with that decision.)

"Did you throw me out of your family because of that, or cut me off from your inheritance, or say I wasn't your daughter any longer because I did some things you didn't like?" A look of utter shock at the very lunacy of the idea crossed his face. "NO! I wouldn't do that!" he said. So I continued. "The Bible uses the illustration that you were BORN into God's family when you believed that Christ died to pay the price for your sins and rose from the dead. God won't throw you out of His family just because you may have done some things He didn't really like either. Birth is a permanent situation. You can't be <u>un</u>born. For all eternity you will be in God's family because you were born into it by faith in Christ. You didn't kick me out of your family when I wasn't perfect and God won't kick you out of His family just because you weren't perfect." Dad didn't say a word, but I watched as that sank in and understanding crossed his face.

I flew back to Vermont and some days later my sister had to make an overnight trip to bring my mother to visit Dad. (The nursing home he was in was quite far from their home.) She later related to me that, when it was time to go, Mom kissed Dad and asked, "When will I see you again?" Dad answered simply,

"In heaven." He somehow knew there wouldn't be another "when" in this life, so he told her exactly "where" he'd meet her. He now had no fears that he wouldn't reach his heavenly Father's home.

The following day my sister was still on the road from returning Mom to her home, so the nursing home staff called me at my office in Vermont. Dad, they advised, was dying very peacefully—completely lucid—still responding to their questions, having no anxiety, no fears. Dad was never one to procrastinate. He was safely home in heaven half an hour before my sister made it back to his side.

> **"As many as receive Christ as Savior [from their sins], to them God gave the right to be the CHILDREN of God, to those who believe in His (Christ's) name: who were BORN...of God." John 1:12-13**

****

Post Script

Date: September 15, 1994

I wrote the above after Dad died in February of 1993. The nursing home just called me in Vermont to tell me that "when" Mom saw Dad again was today at 8:55 a.m. Mom, too, has made her trip home.

The Terrible Parable of The Dark

Diary Entry - 1966: _"I want to sleep in your bed," Jeff, age 4, informed me. Since we didn't want to foster bad sleeping habits in the kids, I tried to discourage the little sprout with: "W-e-l-l-l, you'd have to sleep in the dark!" "That's okay," he hastened to assure me. "I'm not scared of your dark. I'm just scared of MY dark."_

I've never been particularly fond of dark nights either and, since Jeff has long since grown up and has learned to sleep in his own bed at night quite nicely, I'm hoping I relented just that once. I didn't see fit to note my reaction to his request in my diary and I really don't remember what I did. (Oh, cut me some SLACK, you guys. That was over 50 years ago! I have trouble remembering what I did _yesterday._)

There's another kind of "dark" in the world and it's called "the future." It can be terrifying! I know. I used to be apprehensive of even the most _immediate_ future–like what was going to happen in the next five _minutes_–if I had to drive or was being driven anywhere. Unreasoning panic that I wouldn't reach my destination rose in me whenever the car door slammed and the motor started. Ridiculous? Yep. True? Yep. And let's not even TALK about my fears regarding the ghastly situation the world was in. That put me in _total_ turmoil if I thought too much about it. At age 26 I was already at a point in my life where I just couldn't see how the world or I could POSSIBLY survive much longer. "My dark" was getting quite frightening.

I'm no longer afraid to drive across town. I tend to frighten OTHERS with my driving, but I don't count that. A few years ago I set off alone–in the dead of winter–on a 16-hour trip–driving straight through with no sleep–from New York, then across the barren plains of Canada to Michigan in a car that required my stopping along the highway every thirty miles (including during the dead of night) to add several–yes, SEVERAL–quarts of oil to the engine each time. Same woman, but one no longer afraid of "the dark"–immediate or long term.

Why not? I live my life in "God's dark" instead of my own now and it's very peaceful there. I know He can be trusted with my future. What Christ said is true:

> **_"My peace_ I give you; not as the world gives do I give to you. Let not your heart be troubled, neither let it be afraid." John 14:27**

Now, anyone who knows my situation in life is snorting and saying, "Oh, good grief!! Here she is crediting faith in Christ for the peace in her life. Of COURSE she has peace! She's reasonably healthy for an old goat, has a wonderful husband and family, and a home of her own. What more does ANY one person need to have peace?" Well, I had all those things at the time I was neurotic about driving across town, too. It didn't help me then and I know many people today who have it "ALL" and have absolutely no peace in their lives. My heart goes out to them.

My husband and I visited a friend recently–in jail. He has no idea when he'll get out, has lost his job, has only a few possessions left, fewer friends, and has NO IDEA what his future holds for him after he's served his jail time. His comments on his situation? "I know God has a purpose in all this. This will all work out for good somehow." This man has inner peace and has no fear of the future, no matter how dark it appears. He's living in "God's dark" rather than "his dark" and the peace shows in his face.

Now this same man, six months earlier, was an absolute <u>basket case</u> when he realized his life was on a crash course with the local jail. "His dark" was black indeed. So how did he go from basket case to peace? Same way I did. He started looking into the claims of Christ; the "lip-service" faith he had in Christ slipped about 18 inches in a southerly direction, hit his heart, and now actually MEANS something to him. He's studying the Bible with help and encouragement from several Christians God has placed in his path while he's in jail, and now applies to himself—as I do—the verse:

"And we know that ALL things work together for good to them that love God, to those who are the called according to His purpose." Romans 8:28.

Before this man landed in jail, my husband and I had tried on several occasions to get him interested in learning more about Christ, but the message went in one ear and faster out the other. After all, he believed in God, didn't he? In his mind he was sittin' pretty. God really had to "get tough" with him and plug our friend's "out" ear with iron bars (literally) to hold the Word of God in his head long enough for it to grow and send out roots that eventually hit his heart. I believe God has to "get tough" with a lot of us before we listen and, believe me, God knows HOW to get tough. (God's gotten tough with me already. I didn't LIKE it—but it was GOOD for me!)

"...making melody in your heart to the Lord, GIVING THANKS always for ALL THINGS to God the Father in the name of Christ." Eph. 5:20.

*Does our friend LIKE all the things that are happening? NO WAY! Do **I** like everything that comes into my life now that I know it's for my ultimate good? NO WAY!! I'm afraid the "melody I make in my heart" has some real teeth-jarring off-key notes when I first sing it. But eventually I can turn situations I don't like over to the Lord and say, "Okay, Lord. I sure don't understand this one, and I LIKE it even LESS!—but thank you anyway. SOMEHOW good will come from this and I know You and I will get through this together."*

Do you have peace in your life? Whose "dark" are <u>YOU</u> living in?

<u>Update:</u> *This was written several years ago and this friend is now out of jail, has turned his life around, and is now living for Christ!*

The Terrible Parable of Dressing Right

1966 Diary Entry: I was sewing and Jeff, age 4, was cutting up left-over material and laying the scraps on the back of my sweater as I worked at the sewing machine. "I'm making you a dress, mommy," he proudly told me. After much cutting, placing and replacing, he finally told me, "Okay, mommy. Stand up. And if it don't fall off, it's done."

My diary doesn't record what happened when I stood up. Jeff was such a tender-hearted little soul I'm sure I wore his "dress" to avoid hurting his feelings, but I doubt it was very long before bits and pieces began to flutter off and onto the floor. I certainly couldn't have worn it for a special occasion.

Speaking of special occasions, when a friend's son got married, I got in on the hustle and bustle of the event—doing all sorts of jobs for him so he could be sure _everything_ would be PERFECT!

Part of his "everything" included his being certain he and "The Queen Bee" (his pet name for his wife) would be dressed right! He bought a new suit and looked positively regal. But the Queen Bee had to go shopping in several far-off cities before she found the perfect mother-of-the-groom dress. I had considered offering her Jeff's haute couture abilities to save her the frustration of shopping, but since Jeff's tailoring expertise hadn't improved in the intervening 50 years since he made MY dress, I kept my mouth shut.

Now my friend was perfectly willing to buy a suit for himself and a lovely dress for the Queen Bee so they'd be dressed right, but the guests had to buy their OWN duds. No one came dressed like some modern diva's (who shall remain nameless) so no one had to be thrown out on their ear for being inappropriately attired. The wedding was perfect!

This brings to mind a parable from the Bible that had me stumped for many years. In Matthew 22:1-14 Jesus said **"that the kingdom of heaven is like a certain King who arranged a marriage for his son."** When everything was PERFECT, the King sent word through his servants to the guests... **"See, I have prepared my dinner...and all things are ready. Come to the wedding!"** But the guests wouldn't come. (My friend had loyal friends and didn't have this problem of disinterested guests.)

Anyway, it seems the Bible's King HAD no loyal friends. Jesus said, **"the guests made light of the invitation and went their own ways."** Some of those invited even turned hostile and **"...seized the servants of the King and killed them."** (Not all of my friend's guests could go to the wedding, but no one murdered the mailmen that brought the invitations! I like those friends better!)

Now, this murder routine definitely upset the Biblical King and he **"destroyed the murderers and burned up their city."** Then he went looking for other guests and **"sent his servants into the highways and byways to gather together all whom they found, both bad and good, and the wedding was filled with guests."**

So far so good. I understood that the "King" was God the Father who had His "servants," the Jewish prophets and John the Baptist, offer a special relationship with His "Son," Jesus Christ, to His chosen "guests," the Jews. I also understood that when the Jewish nation killed the prophets and John the Baptist, and crucified Christ instead of receiving Him as Savior, God "burned their city" by destroying Jerusalem and scattering the Jewish people throughout the world when Titus attacked in 70 AD. God then turned to the "highways and byways" offering any Jew OR Gentile the chance to accept Christ as Savior. (And since **I'm** a Gentile, I really appreciate that.) If the parable had ended there, I'd have been happy.

BUT...as the Bible so <u>often</u> does to me, it threw me for a loop when it went on to say that during this wedding celebration, **"...the King came in and saw a man who did not have on a wedding garment...and he said to him, 'Friend, how did you come in here without a wedding garment?' And the guest was speechless. Then the King said... 'Bind him hand and foot, take him away, and cast him into outer darkness.' There will be weeping and gnashing of teeth."**

For the longest time I thought this inferred that someone could believe that Jesus died and rose again especially for him, thereby making him a Christian, only to have God meet him at the gates of heaven and REJECT him! And I thought, "But LORD! You said ANYONE can come to the wedding of your Son now! How could You reject someone just because he wasn't DRESSED right?"

But I know God is always fair and realized I was misunderstanding something. I just didn't know what that "something" was. Finally, I learned about wedding traditions of Jesus' day and age. It seems that the King GAVE a proper wedding garment to every guest so they'd be dressed right. (My friend didn't do THAT!) The "Guest" in the parable deliberately chose to REFUSE the proper clothing and wear his OWN outfit. This is why he was "speechless" when he was tossed out on his ear. He had NO excuse for not meeting the King's criteria for entrance and he KNEW it!

Now I understand that when God gives a "robe of righteousness" to anyone who comes to Him through faith in Christ, they'll be "dressed right" for time AND eternity. **"For HE has clothed me with the garments of salvation and HE covered me with the robe of righteousness."** *Isaiah 61:10. People can face eternity dressed in their own duds if they want, but I don't recommend it. Isaiah 64:6 says:* **"...all OUR righteousnesses are as FILTHY RAGS"** *in God's eyes.*

Let's see...what's a winning move here? My friend wouldn't give us ANY clothes; Jeff would give us SCRAPS that would flutter off in a few minutes; our own righteousness dresses us in filthy RAGS; but God dresses us in HIS righteousness for ETERNITY to anyone who'll accept it through faith in Christ. Jesus clued us in when He said **"I am the way, the truth and the life. NO MAN comes to the Father except thru me." John 14:6.**

Not much of a contest, is it?

The Terrible Parable of the Easter Recipe

Most kids imitate what their parents do—or at least imitate what they THINK the parent is doing. Like my child: I was barbecuing and Jeff, age 3, watched as I basted the chicken with a mixture of oil and vinegar. On my next trip to the grill, I found the chicken to be quite moist and the cement around the grill soaking wet. The mystery was solved when I found white-wall tire cleaner sitting innocently beside the oil and vinegar. I had been "assisted" by a very young chef.

Jeff had no idea what he was doing and I'm sure it made absolutely NO SENSE to him, but if mommy's recipe said to put wet stuff on the chicken, it MUST be the right thing for him to do too. And that is why—when I was very young—I believed the Bible was true. No...not because the chicken was wet, but because my <u>parents</u> believed the Bible was true—therefore it <u>must</u> be true.

But it made NO sense to me. Take the Old Testament "recipe" God gave to the Israelites for their last meal (the Passover meal) of lamb before they followed Moses into the desert for 40 years. Get a load of these <u>bizarre</u> cooking instructions from Exodus 12:1-11.

1. *Had to use <u>male</u> lambs or goats.* **Chauvinism? Way back then?**
2. *Had to be blemish free—the very best!* **(Okay with me!)**
3. *Had to be killed at twilight.* **(It'd make more sense to do this in the morning and have all day to cook it. I'll bet a <u>MAN</u> is setting up this time schedule!)**
4. *Had to be roasted in fire—not boiled or eaten raw.* **(No PROBLEM! Raw lamb? Yuck!)**
5. *Had to be eaten with unleavened bread and bitter herbs.* **(Bitter herbs?! I want mint jelly and sweet corn!)**
6. *Had to be roasted with head, legs and even INNARDS intact!* **(You don't CLEAN IT?! And you leave the HEAD on?! You MUST be kidding!!)**
7. *Could not break a single bone of the animal when it was being prepared and roasted.* **(Well, okay, but as it cooks, the joints are all going to sag and the lamb will be way out of shape anyway!)**

Some recipe! I'm not especially fond of fussing in the kitchen, but I'd at LEAST take the time to clean the innards out of the carcass before I roasted it! This lamb recipe would NEVER make it to my "Favorite Recipes" file! But it HAS made it to my "Favorite Photos" album.

You remember those strange 3-D pop-out-at-you-photos that were so popular a while back? It looks like a framed bunch of NOTHING, but if you can focus correctly, a beautiful picture pops out at you and you wonder how you ever missed it at first. The Bible's full of 3-D'ers. When you think about a maze of information just right, a picture pops out at you that you didn't see before. Let me "refocus" the Passover lamb recipe a little differently for you and see if a picture pops out.

1. **Christ is a male.**
2. **Christ had no sin**—*He was perfect—the best God had!*
3. **Christ died at twilight.** *(Remember that the soldiers broke the legs of the two crucified with Christ to hasten their deaths since it was getting close to the Sabbath which began at sundown?*

Christ had died just prior to that or they would have broken His legs also. It was against Jewish law to have anyone hanging on a cross on the Sabbath—which is why they were hustling.)

4. **Fire speaks of judgment** *in Biblical terms. Christ's perfection was judged on that cross, and He was found to be the absolutely perfect substitute who could pay the price God demanded for imperfections (okay, SIN!)—yours and mine. Proof of Christ's perfection was that He rose again from the grave.*

5. **Leaven is always a symbol of sin ("Beware the leaven of the Pharisees",** *etc.) Christ could have no sin, or His substitutionary death would have been imperfect and would NOT have been acceptable to God. Unleavened bread reminded the people that God's "Lamb" would be sinless.*

The bitter herbs? *There was nothing pleasant about the crucifixion. Christ dreaded the ordeal.* **"If it be possible, let this cup pass from me,"** *He prayed. There WAS no other way. Christ said,* **"I am THE way, THE truth and THE life. NO MAN comes to the Father but by me."** *It <u>had</u> to be done, and it was a very bitter experience.*

6/7. **The whole lamb** *pictured the coming Messiah. John said of Jesus,* **"Behold the LAMB of God."** *And Christ's body <u>remained</u> whole on the cross. We're not told, but the Passover lambs were probably killed with one knife wound to the neck (that's how we did it on the farm when I was a kid!) as we know the blood was drained and put on the doorposts of the Israelites' homes. Christ had one sword wound, and His bones were all out of joint from hanging there, but not a single bone was broken!*

*The Jews ate the Passover meal of lamb every year which looked forward to the time <u>God's</u> Lamb would die for them. It was the Passover that Christ ate with his disciples on the night Judas betrayed Him and Jesus **BECAME** the Lamb.*

Are you serving the traditional <u>lamb</u> dinner for Easter this year? Why? "Why?" had been my question for Y-E-A-R-S! I'm not fond of lamb and I could see ABSOLUTELY no reason for serving it. I've known the story of Passover and Easter for half a million years or so, but I never connected the modern-day Easter meal of lamb with the picture the Passover gave mankind 2,000 years ago of God's Lamb. That maze of information FINALLY popped into 3-D focus for me a few years back.

Yeah, I know, I'm slow! My kid didn't understand what I was doing by spraying the chicken, but I definitely did not understand what my heavenly Father was doing with that lamb either!! But it makes SENSE now that I know what's cooking!!

The Terrible Parable of the "Flusher"

***Diary Entry from 1968** - Bryan, age 18 months and Jeff, age 4, were in a nice, warm, soaky bath when Bryan suddenly grabbed the drain lever. Jeff – horror dripping from his voice – gasped, "Oh, Mommy! Bryan's gonna flush it!"*

How many times have you been in a warm, soaky, relaxing time of life when some idiot reached for the drain lever to flush your happiness down the tubes? It's happened to me several times. As a Christian through faith in Christ, I know God has a plan for my life. How can these flushings be in His plan for me if He is my loving heavenly Father?

The Bible says, "For as the heavens are higher than the earth, so are My ways higher than your ways, and My thoughts than your thoughts." Isaiah 55:9. *Oh! God is different from man. He <u>thinks</u> differently and <u>acts</u> differently (and given today's messed up humanity, that's a REAL blessing!) He's also "one of a kind." This theory that "God is in everything and everyone is God" is not something people have picked up from the Bible. Cause that's not in there!*

What IS in there is: **"For I am God and there is NO OTHER: I am God and there is NONE like Me." Isaiah 46:9.** *Now, if God acts, thinks, and IS different from man, and if He has a plan for my life, why doesn't He give me sunshine and happiness instead of flushings? What kind of a Father IS He anyway?*

Surprisingly, He's a lot like our earthly fathers. Tell me something…did your father always make life easy for you when you were a child? Did you have to go to school when you really wanted to stay home and watch TV? Did he make you learn how to clean out the car as well as let you drive it? Did you have to get a part-time job to earn spending money when you got older? It would have been a whole lot easier to turn a faucet attached to your dad's wallet and watch money pour out into your hands instead of working for it. After all, you were a good kid. Some of the things your Dad made you do were pretty hard. And certainly not much fun. You deserved GOOD things!

You know where I'm going with this, don't you? You wouldn't have learned anything by doing nothing! You'd have been useless. Now you have turned into a WONDERFUL… (You are, aren't you? Wonderful, that is?)… person by going through some hard things in your childhood.

The same holds true in the spiritual realm. If God never made us go through some difficulties, we wouldn't learn diddly! We'd never grow up spiritually to be good Christians careful to do good works. **"For we are His workmanship, created in Christ Jesus FOR good works, which God prepared beforehand that we should walk in them." Eph. 2:10.** *Kindly note that we are His "WORKmanship."* It takes a lot of God's WORK to get us whipped into shape. You think you're EASY for God to raise???!!! I'm betting you aren't any easier to raise than I am. And I don't like to brag, but I'm QUITE the handful for Him.

And I'll try to break this next part to you easy…He's not NEAR done raising you yet. Okay, okay…. He's not done with me yet either. But He does have a goal in mind for both of us. **"Those whom He foreknew, He also predestinated to be conformed to the image of His Son…" Romans 8:29.** *That's a rather lofty goal He has set for us, isn't it!!?*

Now answer me something else. Did your Dad make the neighbor kids go to school? Get a job? Help around the house? NEVER! Why should he? They weren't HIS! Same with God. If someone isn't His child *yet by faith...* **("as many as received Him, to them He gave the right to become <u>children</u> of God, to those who believe in His name...who were <u>born</u>...of God." John 1:12, 13)**...*aren't HIS to raise yet. So if your life has been all peaches and cream with no problems to overcome or rise above, don't get cocky! You might not BE God's child yet. If that's your case, I'd look into it if I were you!*

God doesn't raise us JUST with discipline and hard times, of course. The Bible also says that He is a wonderful gift giver. **"Every good gift and every perfect gift is from above and comes down from the Father of lights..." James 1:17.** *He's a really well-rounded Father!*

I accepted Christ as my Savior when I was 28. (I was slow catching on!!) He's given me some wonderful sunshiny gifts since I've been His child and he's also given me some pretty hard flushings—some of which I've failed to accept with the right attitude; some of which I've learned from and grown by. I know I'm in for more gifts and many more flushings of my happiness during the rest of my life. But since I know the flushings will be for my own growth and learning, I'm going to do my best to make Him proud of the way I'll handle those times.

But keep a towel handy for me, will you? I HATE to drip dry.

The Terrible Parable of the Free Lunch

Diary Entry - Feb 28, 1966 *Bryan came into this world three weeks late, according to my reckoning, weighing in at a hefty 9 pounds and 4 ounces. That he had spent those three weeks eating and enjoying those extra meals was confirmed the second day of his life outside the womb when I accidentally dropped the bottle out of his mouth at the noon feeding. All 22 inches of baby boy instantly stiffened out and he emitted a* hor-REND-ous *blood-curdling howl that had nurses popping in from all angles. I knew from their obvious anxiety that they expected to find a baby boy with tiny broken body parts in desperate need of repair. But all Bryan needed was his free lunch bottle popped back into his mouth.*

I'll never know why Bryan was quite so furious as he CLAIMS he doesn't remember the incident. Maybe he knew that sooner or later he'd have to provide his own lunches and feared that I had decided to have him provide them "sooner"...a LOT sooner. Whatever the cause of his tiny temper tantrum, he got a good many free lunches. And, as I recall, he also got several pairs of tennies, a shirt or two, and an education. Actually, the kid cost us a bundle!!

And that brings up a question. Just why do parents WANT these freeloading little kids anyway? They certainly aren't a good financial investment—at least I never made any money from raising three kids. It can't be because they come to us ready to dispense wisdom. I knew one of my kids had very little wisdom at the age of 18 months when the tiny ragamuffin escaped my clutches and took off across a main highway, successfully bringing a semi-truck and a couple cars to a screeching halt! No, kids DEFINITELY don't come pre-filled with wisdom. And they only really *get helpful around the house about the time they move out and go on their own.*

Gee, when it comes right down to it, little kids are a pretty useless bunch, but LOTS of people want them and go to great lengths to get 'em. WHY? for pity sakes? What was MY motive? Was I planning to bill them after they were grown for all the money and time expended—figured at time and a half for everything over eight hours a day and double time for weekends and holidays? NAH! I couldn't count that high! Have I bought myself a motorized rocking chair that I plan to wheel into their living rooms when I get old, gray, and forgetful? Okay....older, grayer and MORE forgetful? PLEASE! I'd drive 'em all crazy in a month.

So what WAS my motive? Same motive I STILL have...just so I could love them and have them send that love back in my direction. Granted, some of my three's childhood antics had me tearing hair at times, but the years I spent raising my children were (and the memories ARE) incredibly precious to me. My children are all grown now, and while not one of 'em run their life exactly *as I might choose to run it FOR them, I'm very proud of the way they turned out!*

Do YOU have any children? Have they cost you anything in time, money, frustration or worry? Are you planning to bill them for the expenses involved and for your services rendered? Admit it! You gave your kids physical life on the "free lunch" basis out of love, didn't you!!

It should come as no surprise to us that God—who is PERFECT love—uses the terminology of "being born" to explain how He gives spiritual life to anyone who chooses to accept it:

"Do not marvel that I said to you, 'You must be born again. That which is born of the flesh is only flesh (human) but that which is born of the Holy Spirit is spirit." John 3:6 and 7.

If we MUST be "born" of the Holy Spirit to get spiritual life, are we talking big maternity ward in the sky here? Hardly! Simply... **"by grace are you saved through faith, NOT of works, lest any man should boast...it is the GIFT of God." (Eph. 2:8)** And that saving faith comes by **"hearing the word of God. (Rom. 10:17)**...which gives us spiritual "birth" since **"those who believe in Christ's name are BORN of God. (John 1:12-13).** (Kindly note!! There won't be anyone up in glory bragging about how wonderful they are. Works don't count toward getting you to heaven...only faith counts!!)

How long does God promise to KEEP you in His family after you're born into it? **"Whoever believes on Christ shall not perish but shall have ETERNAL life." (John 3:15)** ETERNALLY!! This is tough for some people to swallow because they know how NASTY they can be at times and they KNOW–but don't like to ADMIT that eternal life would be a gift they don't really deserve. But check out the amount of physical life that you give to your own precious child. I've yet to hear a parent warn his child at birth, "Okay, kid! Listen up!! I'm your PARENT here. You'll be allowed to live IF you don't have any temper tantrums and IF you always obey me and IF you grow up and make me proud that I'm your parent." If I had said that to Bryan, I would have had to eliminate the cute little guy after only 48 hours of life!

Now, I disciplined all three of my kids whenever I caught them pulling fast ones, and I thought I was pretty good at it...UNTIL they started reminiscing about what they got away with when they were kids!! But I loved them no matter what and never considered trying to un-born them! However, I really, really expected them to grow up physically, get jobs, and turn into productive adults. Thankfully, all three of mine did. God, too, really wants His children to "grow up" spiritually and do the "work" He would like done. **"....those who have believed in Christ should be careful to maintain good works." (Titus 3:8)** Some don't! Regardless of the discipline God hands out to get a child of His back on the right track, some Christian "kids" NEVER mature spiritually or do any decent "work" for Him.

God is all powerful, so He COULD un-born us Christians if He chose to, but that's not what He promises. I Corin. 3:15 says, **"If anyone's work is burned, he will suffer loss** (of rewards); **but he himself will be saved."** We won't get a lot of stars in our crowns as rewards for doing God's will if we're crummy workmen (work-persons?), but He'll keep us safe for eternity after we've accepted His free lunch–no matter what!

Bryan accepted God's spiritual free lunch when he was just a little sprout and he's been chowing down ever since, but God has a HUGE lunch table and He's got room for you–IF you're hungry!!

The Terrible Parable of God's Family Business

Lately I've been thinking about God's handicaps. Now, I realize people rarely think of God as "handicapped," but He's dealing with multiple and terrible handicaps, and one of the worst is…ME.

*Here we have an omniscient, omnipresent, omnipotent God. **"When I consider the heavens, the work of Your <u>fingers</u>…" Psalm 8:3.** Creating the universe was "finger play" for Him! THINK about that for a minute. God started with nothing and "doodled" a universe into existence! How many of you have doodled (let's go easy on here here) a <u>cloud</u> into existence lately? A star? What about one tiny little mountain? No? Then we're talking real POWER here! How can He possibly be handicapped??? Easy. He's running a "family" construction business.*

Anyone who is involved in a human family can understand the handicaps involved in having family members do ANYTHING! You could do most jobs that your young children "help" you with quicker—and with less frustration—yourself. As my old diary reflects…

> **…Jeff, at 2 years, was not very articulate, so he stood by the refrigerator chattering and pointing. I thought he wanted a piece of fudge (which he loved) but he pushed it aside. He wanted the box of tile that was on top of the refrigerator so he could "help" his dad tile the bathroom. He handed them to his dad "one…at…time" as he put it, slowing his dad's progress nearly to a standstill."**

Sound familiar? Sure. Why do parents and people with family businesses encourage family members' participation? They have fond hopes that SOME day the children will be mature enough to be a help rather than a hindrance. Many times that happens, but many times—approximately a day and a half after they become really mature and helpful—kids fly the coop and go to live on their own. And you have to start training someone else for their job. That's life.

*I was "born" into God's family through faith in Christ 50 years ago…. **"as many as received Christ are…. born of God…" John 1:12, 13.** And I've been QUITE a handicap to Him in His "family construction business" ever since. He only has one project under construction right now—a rather unique church. He laid the cornerstone first, of course, about 2,000 years ago: **"Jesus Christ Himself being the chief cornerstone…" Eph. 2:20.** God Himself is the Master Mason and daily He adds bricks one at a time to form the superstructure: **"And the Lord added to the church daily…" Acts 2:47.** He's going to a lot of trouble to build this church because it's special. It's for His Son. He's building it slowly, and in a rather peculiar shape **"…Christ is head over all the things to the church, which is His body. Eph. 1:23**…a body-shaped church…and He's using "living bricks."*

SO! God is building a body for Christ. Christ is the "head" which means He's the brains of the outfit and in control. Your head controls YOUR body, right? And your body doesn't resent being controlled. God needs "living bricks" to become His "arms," "hands," "feet," "fingers" and "toes" that work together as a "body" to carry out His plans. It's MOST helpful to Him if His "body parts" work in harmony with the "Head."

*How does He GET humans to be "living bricks" in this unique structure? Same way He got me. One of God's older "bricks/body parts/children" acted as His sales rep and delivered the "sales pitch." But instead of asking me to buy anything, she told me how God wanted to <u>give</u> me the free gift of salvation… **"By grace***

you are saved through faith…it is the GIFT of God" Eph. 2:8. *When I eventually understood and believed that Christ died for me, I was a new "brick/body part" and became part of….or "in" Christ's body.* **"For we are His workmanship, created IN Christ Jesus" Eph. 2:10.** *Just that quick, God had grabbed up His trowel, slapped permanent mortar on me, and cemented me into Christ's body/church. When I started causing Him problems, He sighed and shook His head. He could see I was going to be a trouble maker who had few plans to cooperate with the "Head." But it was too late…the mortar was permanent.*

I didn't cause big problems immediately. I started out small and whined that I didn't like my lowly spot in His body. I wanted to do GREAT things…wanted to be a "mouth." "No, Carolyn, that's part of the Head and that position is TAKEN!" God told me sternly. "Besides, the mouth you have now causes Me enough trouble. I need you to be part of the fingers."

He graciously didn't tell me I was barely of any use to Him even as a lowly finger since I hadn't grown enough spiritually to learn the "family business" yet. So I chomped at the bit to be doing something "more important," but did start studying and learning more and tried to hand him "living bricks" "one…at… time." However, if the truth were known, my "help" probably slowed construction in my area of the body to a dead stop!

Eventually, I hit the rebellious teenage years and, when some problems came into my life, I blamed HIM instead of taking any responsibility myself. I was such a bad representative for His business that He shelved me until I got over being rebellious and angry. I was a useless member of the family business. He tolerated my bad attitude for a while, but finally got tired of my pouting and grumbling and took me for a couple well-deserved trips to the woodshed. I got the message!! Straightened up my act. Decided to follow what the "brains of the outfit" wanted me to do again.

Once again He told me, "Carolyn, you're part of the FINGERS! See if you can't be of some small use to Me there! This is part of the work I prepared for you to do after you became My child/body part/sales rep." **"…we are His workmanship, created <u>IN</u> Christ Jesus <u>FOR</u> good works, which God <u>prepared beforehand</u> that we should walk in them." Eph. 2:10.**

I've been typing away ever since…a sales rep for God's gift of salvation, and trying to provide Him with living bricks for His structure one…at…time. I MAY even mature and get good at this job. But do you know what's going to happen then? I'll be so old that I'll fly the coop of this earth and go to live with Him. And He'll have to start training another "body part" to take my place on earth. That's life! (and death).

In the meantime, how about it? Are you one of God's bricks through faith in Christ and working to bring God "living bricks" for Christ's body? If not, come on in! The mortar's fine!!

The Terrible Parable of "I Just Don't Understand"

Bryan, my youngest, had NO thirst for book knowledge. Never studied. For 12 years I got ..."Honest, mom. I don't HAVE any homework." Drove me nuts! But he learned some things just by living with a minuscule allowance when he was nine:

> **"Bryan sat in deep silence as he rode home with me after a shopping trip. The toy trucks he wanted to buy had sported price tags that his paltry budget simply could not handle. Still deep in thought he finally asked, "Mom, why do they call it an 'allowance' when it doesn't 'allow' you to DO anything?"**

*My child was trying to understand. Then he turned into a teenager and understood EVERYTHING for several years. But he's now in his 50's and once again there are things that make no sense to him. I'm almost 80, don't understand LOTS of things, and don't even CARE about most of 'em. One thing I DO want to understand, though, is the Bible. "Good Luck," right? Gifted scholars who have spent their entire lifetimes studying that Book in the original languages don't understand everything and here **I** come diddly-bopping along–wanting to understand the infinite God of the universe! Fortunately, God knew from eternity past that I was going to pester the stew out of Him for answers even though I was somewhere out in left field when most of the brains were passed out, so He took pity on me. He gave me a special teacher...*

> **"...the Holy Spirit, whom the Father will send in My name, will <u>TEACH</u> you all things..." John 14:26.**

And knowing that I couldn't be trusted without my teacher and would need heavy-duty tutoring my whole live-long life, God provided that my Tutor would be the permanent "live-in" variety:

> **"He will give you another Helper, that He may abide with you <u>forever</u>, the Spirit of truth....will be <u>IN</u> you." John 14:17**

I had been puzzling over Biblical "oddities" from the time I was just a little sprout, but God didn't give me my Tutor until I accepted Christ as Savior when I was 28. He couldn't. He has rules that He follows and His rule about getting me the Tutor says I had to hear that Christ died to pay the price for my sins and rose again; then I had to believe it; and THEN I'd get the Tutor:

> **"You trusted in Christ AFTER you heard the gospel...and HAVING BELIEVED, you were SEALED with the Holy Spirit of promise." Eph. 1:13.**

Even WITH my Tutor, I'm not the sharpest pencil in the box, but I DID understand something the other day that had been rolling around in my brain since I was a scrawny kid. (I WAS scrawny a very long time ago. I've got pictures to prove it! I digress.)

You remember Moses. When you were just little I'll bet you were told about baby Moses going sailing in the river all alone at the tender age of three months. Cute story. Touching. Were you ever told about Moses killing an Egyptian and hiding the very dead body in the sand? Did you know that's why Moses ran to Midian and hid in the desert 40 years raising sheep? He was afraid of being caught and punished. (Ex. 2:11-15) NOT cute. Not touching.

After 40 years, God sought Moses out and asked him to lead the Israelites into the Promised Land. It was time to lead men instead of sheep and, after hemmmmming and hawwwwwing for a while, Moses agreed. But he ran into a snag leading men through the desert – the people were thirsty and the river was dried up. God told Moses, **"STRIKE the rock, and water will come out of it, that the people may drink." (Exodus 17:6***) Moses struck the rock and water poured out. The people were happy; Moses was happy; God was happy.*

THEN!!!! The Israelites came to another place in the desert where there was no water. God told Moses, **"SPEAK to the rock... and it will yield its water." (Num. 20:8)** *Welllllll, Moses was in a cranky mood and instead of speaking to the Rock, he struck it twice with his rod. "God was HIGHLY offended at this and told Moses and Aaron,* **"...you shall <u>not</u> bring this assembly into the land which I have given them." (Num. 20:12).**

Good Grief!! God knew Moses hit and KILLED a man, but chose Moses to lead His people out of Egypt anyway. Then, because Moses hit a ROCK, he's denied the honor of leading the people into the Promised Land!! God is more upset about Moses hitting a rock than killing a man? EXPLAIN this to me! I just don't understand.

Then I was clued in that the Bible often uses a rock as a picture of Christ. The rock in the desert gave water to satisfy man's physical thirst. Christ promised He would give "living water" (or the Holy Spirit) to satisfy man's <u>spiritual</u> thirst. We know the rock refers to Christ because Paul says of the water-from-rock incidents in the desert: **"...your fathers...all drank of that spiritual Rock...and that Rock was Christ." (I Cor. 10:1-4).**

How often was Christ (the Rock) crucified–(STRUCK)–before the Holy Spirit ("Living Water") was given? ONCE! God told Moses to strike the Rock ONE time. After that he was to SPEAK to the rock. Christ will never be crucified or "struck" again. Now, we only need to "speak"–acknowledge Christ as Savior–and we are freely given the Holy Spirit (God's living water). Moses's temper tantrum ruined what would have been a perfect picture–hundreds of years in advance–of the cross and the giving of the Holy Spirit. No <u>wonder</u> God was upset.

Wow! Thanks, Lord! I understand that one. But, you know, there are plenty more "pictures" in the Old Testament that I haven't figured out yet.

Soooooooooooooooooooooo, just what did You mean when.....

The Terrible Parable of "Thank You, Lord. I HATE It!"

Diary Entry 1968: _We went to a family reunion in a park that had no restroom but which was "blessed" with an ill-maintained outhouse. My mother was very undemocratically elected to take a 3-year-old and Bryan, age 2, on a potty break. Mom came back laughing and reported that the 3-year-old complained: "P-U! This place stinks! Is this a cow place? I'm getting OUT of here!! But Bryan held a slightly different opinion. His comment? – "This place stinks! I L-I-I-I-K-E stinks!"_

 I read this entry in my diary again and had to grin, but anyone who was not raised in the hey-day of drafty, dilapidated outhouses–as I was–has no point of reference for this and should be extremely <u>grateful</u>, by the way!

 Here were two kids in a less-than-ideal situation with totally opposite attitudes. And for once, I can use MY kid's attitude as the proper one to strive for when events in our lives don't resemble roses.

 A while back a fine young Christian teen in our church was badly injured in an accident. I know the mother of this teenager very well and know that she has bathed her offspring in constant prayer since way BEFORE the day he was born. Here are Godly people who are going through a world of hurt. And the question surfaces…"Why is God allowing this trial to come into the lives of His own children?" It sent me scurrying to my Bible to find some of the reasons God's people suffer. I haven't a CLUE as to ALL the reasons God has for allowing suffering or why God allowed this accident, but I found some interesting insights:

 I found Joseph was hated by his own brothers who sold the poor kid into slavery at the tender age of 17. He was taken to Egypt, unjustly jailed for years on the whim of a scorned, angry WOMAN, but rose to power in Egypt in time to save his whole family from starvation. Joseph had to wait <u>20 years</u> before he understood how God was working through the evil that had come to him. We read that Joseph said: **"As for you,** (Joseph's brothers) **you meant evil against me; but God used it for good…to save many people alive." Gen. 50:20**. I'll betcha he'd wondered why he was going through horrible trials a good MANY times. God didn't keep Joseph from falling into evil hands, but He did work out His purposes for good <u>around</u> and <u>in spite of</u> the evil. (God could even work around an angry, scorned WOMAN!! No mere mortal EVER manages that!!!)

 Then Moses comes to mind. Moses somehow knew he was supposed to deliver the Jewish people from Egyptian bondage (the Bible neglects to say HOW he knew), and killed an Egyptian in his hurry to get started on his mission. BUT…he hadn't bothered to check the <u>Lord's</u> timetable and had to scurry into the desert to keep his tail feathers out of Pharaoh's angry reach. There he spent 40 years as a shepherd tending sheep. Wasted time? God had deserted him? No WAY! God allows all of us (evil <u>and</u> good) free will to run our lives and <u>some</u> of our choices prove to be less than wise, causing us considerable problems. But God used Moses' choices to train him in desert survival techniques. Would you go camping in the desert if YOUR leader had no desert survival knowledge? Moses knew the desert inside and out by the time he was asked to lead millions of Israelites through those dunes. It may take years for God to work through our choices too.

Job is the sufferer everyone knows about. He was "a 'perfect' man" who God used as a witness to others by allowing the poor man to undergo all <u>sorts</u> of troubles. (I must admit, I used to shudder and think: "Oh, Lord! Don't use ME for this type of witnessing!" But I'm totally safe. The older I get, the more I realize I fall WAY short of perfection.) I like the first and last chapters of the Book of Job, but in between are 40 BORING chapters of folderol where Job's "friends" try to analyze his suffering. The narrative is full of accusations, weeping, wailing, and much gnashing of teeth. I'll TELL ya...with "friends" like his, Job didn't need enemies! But Job does show us the emotions that a suffering person goes through. Many Biblical incidents are so condensed that feelings are never recorded. You get the impression God's people went through <u>horrendous</u> events with nary a tear, never getting angry, never worried; never questioning, "Why, Lord?" It's nice to know Job had wild swings of emotion like I have when I'm feeling abused.

Have you ever really thought of Noah as suffering? He never complained...that we read about anyway. But can you imagine Noah's thoughts when God tells him: "Okay, Noah. Here's the story. I'm going to destroy your home, your fields, and all your livestock except a couple of each type animal. Not only that, you are going to preach the way of salvation to your neighbors for <u>one</u> <u>hundred</u> years. But don't bother starting a church, because you'll make no converts...they'll just poke fun at you. Oh!.. and by the way, while you're preaching, you and your family are going to build a floating zoo. I KNOW there's no lake anywhere around for you to float it in, Noah. Don't worry about the small stuff. I'll handle that end of it. I'm not angry with you, Noah, but I've HAD IT with the unbelievers. This is how I've chosen to bring judgment on them and save just your family."

So Noah preached, built the floating zoo, and tolerated verbal abuse from the unbelievers. Then came the day when God said, "Okay, Noah. Load everything into the zoo. By the way, did I tell you that you're the head zoo keeper?" <u>NOW!</u> ...you can tell me that the ark was well ventilated and wasn't odorous as some Bible commentaries insist, but you're talking to a FARM girl here. There were cows and pigs and sheep in our "well-ventilated" barns too. And, BELIEVE ME!!! you didn't have to <u>ask</u>, "Is this a cow place??" You KNEW!! I'll bet Noah told his family more than once, "Boy, this situation stinks!" But at least he knew the REASON for it.

Are you God's own child through faith in Christ's death, burial, and resurrection? Are you in a situation you don't understand where you're saying, "Is this a COW place? I want OUT of here!?" Don't know about you, but I've never yet been able to say, "This stinks! I <u>L-I-I-I-K-E</u> stinks!" The best I've been able to say <u>so</u> far is, "Boy, Lord, this stinks! I hate it, I HATE it, I HATE IT!!! But thank you. I know You can work around and through this. I'll hang in there with You because I know You're hanging in there with me."

BUT!!! Is it easier to <u>know</u> the right attitude than to HAVE it? You BETCHA!!!!

"<u>ALL</u> things work together for good to them that love God..." Rom. 8:28

The Terrible Parable of the Jesus Tree

__Old Diary Entry - December 19, 1965.__ I put up the Christmas tree today and Jeff, who is the ripe old age of "almost three," put on the unbreakable ornaments. Puffed up with pride at his own importance, he diligently decorated, carefully choosing where each ornament should be placed. Finally he announced that he was finished. And he had done a magnificent job...hanging 11 ornaments on one branch, 5 on the branch right next to it and a couple clustered closely in the vicinity. The rest of the tree was totally bare.

Those were fun Christmases—when my three kids were small and so excited about everything! I enjoyed watching them decorate the tree and make HUGE messes in the kitchen as they each took possession of one-third of the cookie dough to make the UGLIEST decorated Christmas sugar cookies you can imagine! The memories of the happy chattering that went on around that kitchen table as they rolled and re-rolled cookie dough, ate more cookie dough than they baked, and left trails of colored sugar across the floor bring nostalgic smiles these many years later (Is there ANYTHING worse than stepping on spilled sugar?)

Now, however, if it weren't for having a husband that really, REALLY wants a tree put up, I'd probably just "Bah, Humbug!" the whole decorating-the-tree routine. These days it seems to take EFFORT to drag out the decorations. And don't you find it annoying to find stray pine needles in weird places the next July? Well, I do. Besides...Christmas has gotten so utterly COMMERCIAL these days. We're supposed to be celebrating the birth of Christ and I often feel the crowd of commercialism has elbowed Christ right out of view at His own birthday party.

In 1995 I was even grumpier than usual because we had opened a business. Opening the business didn't make me grumpy, but Doug's confronting me with a hard fact of business sure did! Hard fact: we HAD to decorate our huge showroom for the season. I knew I'd lose, but I fought 'im to the BITTER end! "Do we HAVE to have a tree? Decorate ALL these windows? You GOTTA be kidding??" I whined, but of course, I lost all the battles and found myself buying decorations that I really, REALLY didn't want to put up.

I was scowling at some particularly gaudy decorations in Aisle 12 of K-Mart when, for some reason, my mind wandered off on one of its tangents and I began to "see" Christmas trees as a picture of Christ and His true Church. Oh, I hear you, "She's really lost it THIS time!!" (Well, you're right, so you purists out there are gonna have to cut me some slack in this analogy, okay? It's HARD to turn one pine tree into a whole Church.)

But look at it sorta this way...a Christmas tree grows from one tiny seed that produces a single spike that points straight up—ignored and insignificant except in the eyes of the person who planted that seed and who now tends that new growth. But, given time, that single spike grows into a beautiful pine that we bring into our home and make absolutely beautiful with lights and _evenly-spaced_ ornaments (since we don't have Jeff's assistance these days!)

Jesus, in His stint here on earth as God/Man, grew from a single seed of a woman. He's that single "spike" that points us "straight up" to God. He, too, was ignored and the world considered Him insignificant. Only a few—including Mary and Joseph, the shepherds and wise men, and good old Simeon—truly understood and believed that Jesus was the Messiah. My mind's eye sees them as the first tiny branches in the mighty "pine" of Christ's Church.

For the next thirty years of Jesus' life, no one else knew…or cared…who He was. **"…even His brothers did not believe in Him." (John 7:5)** and ridiculed Him when He began to announce His mission on this grungy earth. Jesus' brothers knew Him intimately but apparently saw nothing significant about Him the whole thirty years they lived together in the same household and didn't believe who He was until He rose from the grave!! I couldn't believe they were so dumb!! So, since this is MY analogy and MY parable, I saw their branches as somewhat insignificant too.

THEN I realized that I grew up believing in God and knew that Christ died on the cross, but was 28 before I understood that His death and resurrection provided my salvation. It was only then that I first saw something really significant about Him and became a "branch." So…humbled, I upgraded His brothers' and sisters' branches to prominent branches in His tree. (Do you suppose I'll have to apologize to them in glory some day??? Sheesh!!) The "Jesus Tree" has been growing new branches for nearly 2,000 years now and the current number of branches is beyond my tiny mind's ability to even imagine.

The lights on Christmas trees now remind me that Christ said of Himself, **"I have come as a light into the world that whoever believes in Me should not abide in darkness." John 12:46.** He gives us His spiritual light and, in return, asks Christians to… **"Let YOUR light so shine before men…" Matt. 5:16.** I wonder…does my branch have any lights on it that are shining for Him? Or are all my bulbs burned out so that my life shows forth none of His light for others to see?

And then there are the ornaments that remind me that God wants Christians' lives **"adorned… with good works." I Tim. 2:10.** I'm so BAD at being good. I fear several of my ornaments have fallen off my branch and lay shattered on the ground. I'm certainly glad that living branches don't fall out of trees, or I'd surely lose my salvation (my branch) as well as make a mess of some of my "good works."

As you gaze at your Christmas tree this year, I hope you'll see more than branches with beautiful ornaments and twinkling lights. And may the most beautiful branch on your tree represent how God and the world sees you.

Merry Christmas!!

The Terrible Parable of Justice

Diary Entry - 1970 **_The wind was really howling and Bryan, age 4, came in rubbing his eye and whining: "That wind blew sand in my eye!" "Nasty old Wind!" I sympathized. "Yeh!' he agreed, and then added with great vehemence, "And if I find the man that's <u>blowing</u> that wind, I'm gonna KICK 'im!"_**

Here was my kid with sand in his eye, vengeance in his heart, ready and able to mete out JUSTICE—just as soon as he could find the bad guy!

Justice. Everyone wants to find the bad guy and get justice if they are innocent of accused wrongdoing or if they are a victim of some OTHER guy's wrongdoing. But don't talk justice to the actual bad guy. The last thing a guilty person wants is JUSTICE delivered by a cop, a court of law—OR an angry four year old!

Personally, I'm not what most people consider a "heavy-duty bad guy," but I DO tend to misread speed limit signs. I'd SWEAR they say: "Speed Limit - 35 M.P.H. - Except for Carolyn." And that is how I've been known to drive—UNLESS I spot a cop car or a cop spots me and closes in for the kill!

Lordie, Lordie, I do hate those flashing blue lights! When those cops come up to the window of my car and give me the usual routine—"Do you have ANY IDEA how fast you were <u>going</u> back there?" I'm not thinking, "Oh, how fortunate! I'm guilty; I've been caught; and now I'm gonna get JUSTICE here!" No Way!! I'm hoping this cop is gonna have MERCY on me regardless of the fact that my actions were totally wrong and I rightfully deserve a ticket.

If the cop isn't feeling merciful that day and I get a ticket, SOMEBODY's got to pay! Now the Court won't care whose money they get, but there aren't a WHOLE lot of people in this world who're going to fork over their hard-earned cash to pay for what I've deliberately and knowingly done wrong. And why should they? THEY weren't speeding!!

But! Suppose some rich, handsome Prince Charming (or a poor-but-handsome, long-suffering Husband Charming) says, "I'll have mercy on you and pay that fine for you, Carolyn." Do you think I'm gonna humble myself and accept the offer? YOU BETTER BELIEVE IT!!! (I have been stopped SEVERAL times and after 52 years got my FIRST TICKET this year!!! After 52 years of mercy, I got JUSTICE!! I'm driving much slower now!)

I'd rather have mercy instead of justice from <u>God</u> too if the Bible is true!! You know, it's no wonder some people don't like reading that Book a whole lot. So many parts of it are so blunt and uncaring!! It regards people's feelings not at ALL! It calls even nearly perfect ME a sinner**!! "ALL have sinned and come sort of the glory of God." (Rom. 3:23)** The NERVE!!!!

Not only does the Bible bad-mouth me and say I'm a sinner, it says I've come up short of having God's glory. Now, granted, being God or having His glory is a rather lofty goal, but no one likes to come short of ANY goal. And if we have to come up short, then we only want to be a teensy BIT short so no one will notice. I've tried to find a passage that says I'm only a teensy bit short of being God, but instead I find:

**"These seven things the Lord HATES:...a proud look** (Arrghh! Welllllll, sometimes!!)**....a lying tongue** (Not often, Lord, but I gotta admit I've shaved the truth here and there when it was absolutely, positively <u>necessary</u>.)**...hands that shed innocent blood** (Haven't—but the thought did appeal to me a couple times in my 78 years)**...a heart that devises wicked plans** (But Lord! I rarely go THROUGH *with 'em)...**feet swift in running to mischief** (I'm getting WAY too old for this one any more)...**a false witness who speaks lies and one who causes discord among the brethren...**" **Proverbs 6:16-19**.*

YOU! You out there! Read that list again and be honest with me. Do you know anyone who doesn't come miserably short of perfection?

*Then—again with absolutely NO finesse—the Bible says, "**The <u>wages</u> of sin** (what you actually "earn!") **is death...**" Coming short of God's perfection warrants "death!" That's a heavy-duty fine that somebody's got to pay! You know anyone who'll pay your speeding tickets, let alone lay down his life for YOU???? Yeah! Yeah, I do!!"*

*"**While we were yet sinners, Christ died FOR** (or INSTEAD OF) **us.**" **Romans 5:8**. Gee! Suddenly that Bible is just FULL of finesse. I LIKE the sound of that! And then, "**Not by works of righteousness which WE have done, but according to His MERCY He saved us through Jesus Christ.**" **Titus 3:5.**

Know anyone who needs mercy instead of justice? Don't let 'em anywhere near mean little 4-year-olds who may be wearing steel-toed sneakers—and tell 'em about Christ.

Mom's Trip Home

Mom never liked to travel. She didn't stand up well under the rigors of suitcases, driving long hours, and sleeping in strange motel beds with lumps in all the wrong places. To my memory, we attempted only one family trip—a short one to Niagara Falls. And that ended with all of us coming home earlier than planned—mom riding lying down in the back seat of the car, totally fatigued.

After I moved to the "Great Northeast" several years ago, I urged her and dad to come out for a visit, but my requests were gently but firmly refused with reference usually made to the lack of convenient restroom facilities during any drive or flight out—the availability of bathrooms at the rear of airplanes cutting absolutely NO ice with her.

No, mom was definitely NOT a traveler. But one trip that every human being is forced to make is the one through that valley named "The Shadow of Death." Dad made a peaceful trip through that deep, dark valley in February of 1993 and while mom was grateful that he had a peaceful "trip," she was thoroughly unhappy that she had been left behind. We talked about it several times and she would always conclude, "I'll just have to wait."

Mom didn't look forward to her trip through that Valley of the Shadow of Death. No one does. Valleys are, by definition, low points and death rarely travels the high road. Death was decreed upon us by God as the route out of this world after sin entered it. But our God is gracious to us. He gave the actual death His righteousness required in payment for our sins to Christ to bear. **("The wages of sin is death...")** *Romans 6:23* **"...while we were still sinners, Christ died for** *[INSTEAD OF]* **us."** *Romans 5:8) So Christians are only required to travel through the "shadow" of death. Shadows can be incredibly dark and frightening, but there is always light on the other side or there could be no shadow cast. Christ said,* **"I am the light of the world."** *He is the light behind the "shadow" and all those who trust in Christ will pass safely through that dark time.*

For a year and a half mom slowly traveled toward that dark valley and finally reached its entrance. She paused there for several days. During this pause one of her seven brothers came to her bedside. As he and his wife listened, mom mumbled incoherently then she said very clearly, "I hear you, Gerald." ("Gerald" was [and still IS] dad's name) She mumbled again, then added—again very clearly—"You have to be patient." Two days later she peacefully traveled through the dark shadow and into the light of Christ beyond.

Was mom's last earth-bound conversation with dad just coincidence—the ramblings of the dying? Or was it a beautiful gift of assurance given to her family and friends when the door to heaven cracked open for her to hear dad impatiently calling her to hurry into the light beyond that shadow of death—on to a better life purchased for her by Christ's death on that cross and His resurrection from the dead 2,000 years ago?

"For me to live is Christ and to die is gain." Phil 1:21

The Terrible Parable of the Big Mouth

<u>*DIARY ENTRY–1973:*</u> *We were on vacation at a dude ranch and had gotten to know some of the other "dudes." Bryan, age 7, was asking me, "Do you know Charlie? She's the one with the big mouth." "Oh," I cringed, glancing around to see if Charlie was within earshot. "Don't TELL her she has a big mouth. You'll make her feel bad." "Well," Bryan amended, "It's not really SOOO big. And anyway, she doesn't USE it to yell with."*

I used my mouth, which is admittedly "big," <u>often</u> in raising my three children. And yes, Bryan will be happy to tell you about instances when I used my mouth to "yell with"–at HIM. However, that was YEARS ago, and now he's <u>perfect…</u> (Just ask him. He'll be happy to confirm that.)… and my mouth doesn't have much reason to yell. I have, however, found other uses for it. It does a lot of talking and once in a while I allow chocolate or cheese to enter that mouth. Then that mouth gets to whine because cheese or chocolate gives me a migraine!

One thing I truly do NOT like my mouth to do is to lie. But yesterday I listened from a distance as my mouth lied to my boss! (Notice how I'm taking no responsibility for this? Dumb mouth–went out on its own and did something stupid!) It had NEVER lied to my boss before. Even when I've pulled something incredibly moronic in my job, I've cringed and squirmed, but always told him the truth about it. But a couple of my boss's friends wanted to play a joke on him and asked me to tell a certain lie–an inconsequential lie, but a lie nonetheless–and I went along with the gag.

Since I'd never lied to him before, my boss swallowed my story hook, line, and sinker and came through BEAUTIFULLY with the hoped-for reaction. But I was suffering!! My conscience was doing a violent tap dance on my heart. After about 30 seconds of watching him "react," I couldn't stand it any longer, spoiled the joke, and told him the truth. Why? The only way to have a really good business relationship (or any other kind) is for the individuals involved to be able to totally rely on the other's truthfulness. I didn't want to jeopardize his future trust in the truthfulness of words flowing from my big mouth for the sake of a lousy gag!

The Bible says God has a mouth. I think He'd prefer to use it to smile with rather than to "yell with," but He can, and does, "yell" when the situation demands it. He's HAD to "yell" at me a few times to get me back on the straight and narrow since I tend to be a wayward "child," but one thing He NEVER does is lie to me or anyone else! The Bible says: **"…God, who CANNOT lie, promised before time began…" Titus 1:2** and **"…it is IMPOSSIBLE for God to lie…" Hebrews 6:18.** Notice when He started promising truthful things? BEFORE time began. Interesting thought.

Has God made good on all those truthful promises? Nope! NOPE??? That's right–NO! You and I only have, at best,100 years to make good on promises that come out of our mouths, but God has <u>considerably</u> longer. He promised Adam and Eve that a "Seed" (Christ) would crush Satan's head but it was four THOUSAND years before Christ was born to fulfill that promise. ALL God's promises WILL come to pass, but in HIS time, not ours.

God has given many promises that apply to Christians today, however, I'm not overly thrilled with some of 'em. For instance, He says, **"…all who desire to live godly in Christ Jesus WILL suffer persecution." II Tim. 3:12.** I could have lived a LONG time without wanting to know–or <u>experience</u>

that! If I'm God's very own precious child, shouldn't He PROTECT me from everything bad? Unfortunately, no! But He also tells me, **"...the sufferings of this present time are not worthy to be compared with the GLORY which shall be revealed in us." Romans 8:18.** *That's VERY comforting. Believers WILL be rewarded in His time...er, make that "in His eternity" for living a life pleasing to Him in this world.*

God isn't going to ensure that I'm "well heeled" financially while I struggle through this world either! However, if I give back a portion of my income to Him, He promises that He will **"...supply all my need." Phil. 4:19.** *I hear my mouth whine, "But LORD!!! I want..." And He stops me in mid-whine with, "Do you see anything in that verse that says you'll get all your WANTS?"*

Some Christians are wealthy but, so far, being weighed down with riches hasn't posed an immense PROBLEM in my life. But I AM rich in other ways. I possess the peace Christ spoke of when he said: **"These things I have spoken to you that, in Me, you may have peace. In the world you will have tribulation;** *(There He goes again with that "trouble" stuff)* **... but be of good cheer, I have overcome the world." John 16:33.** *I have that "peace that passes understanding" that Christ gives even when I get upset occasionally over trials I'm passing through. And I have the joy that salvation brings. I don't care HOW rich you are, you can't buy inner peace and joy. I know, 'cause I didn't always have them and I notice a BIG difference, thank you very much.*

God promised through Zechariah's mouth in the 6th century B.C: **"Behold, your King is coming to you; He is just and having salvation, lowly and riding on a donkey, a colt, the foal of a donkey." Zechariah 9:9.** *HUNDREDS of years later, Christ finally rode into Jerusalem on Palm Sunday—as God's "lamb" that provided the means for our salvation. His reign as "King" is STILL in the wings—awaiting God's timing. God's slow, but He's never <u>late</u>.*

Two THOUSAND years ago believers were promised, **"The Lord Himself will descend from heaven with a shout...and the dead in Christ will rise first. Then we who are alive and remain shall be caught up together with them in the clouds to meet the Lord in the air. And thus we shall always be with the Lord." I Thess. 4:16-17.** *And I'll bet He can "shout" LOUD!! Yea! But! We're STILL waiting for this one to be fulfilled.*

I'm old, silver-haired and forgetful. Bryan is still young, golden-haired and can remember things! No one should be surprised that <u>I'm</u> looking forward to this event, but Bryan readily admits he's looking forward to it too. That's 'cause, when this promise is fulfilled, Christ won't "use His mouth to yell with." He'll greet us in glory and His <u>smiling</u> mouth will say...

"Welcome Home!"

The Terrible Parable of the Pray-er

We were visiting with some family members recently and they served lunch on the patio. No one prayed—including me. Doug's nephew was amazed! And he let me know it: "This is the first time we've ever eaten without you saying a prayer!"

Arghhhhh!! A heretic is in your midst!!! A closeted not-EVERY-meal-pray-er, born-again, died-in-the-wool, Bible-thumping Christian has been forcibly OUTED!! Now, everyone knows that if I'm a REAL Christian I wouldn't put a bite of food in my mouth at mealtime without saying grace. Right? But there I was—eating without a prayer. Where did my Christianity go awry? It's probably my parents' fault. Perhaps my mother was domineering and my father a wishy-washy wimp. I probably was misunderstood as a child and was traumatized by a cow running amuck in the barnyard at Granddad's house. It certainly can't be MY fault in this day and age of blame-anyone-except-the-perpetrator. I know my rights!!

Now, I'm all FOR praying at mealtime. I know there must be many Christians who offer beautiful heartfelt prayers at every meal. Why am I such a rebel? Well, it seems to be OK to eat snacks between meals without praying, so I get confused. Maybe NO ONE is thankful for junk food. Or is it a necessity to pray because the food is sitting on a table instead of being consumed in a standing position?

Am I to be more vocal with my thanks for my food than for my clothing? No one has EVER been amazed that I haven't offered a prayer of thanks when I don my winter duds before braving an outing in Vermont in February (though many times I do—not with head bowed, but with head tucked deep in my furry collar!) Isn't clothing as necessary as food—especially in Vermont? And I've turned up the thermostat MANY times without anyone being surprised that I didn't bow my head for a moment of thanks for the heat.

Many times I've thanked the Lord because the window panes let in the light but keep out the rain during a thunderstorm...and looked at the ceiling and thanked Him that there was still one there. I'm especially thankful for plastic curtains that keep the shower water IN the shower and for the fact that we have an abundant supply of good water. (Although it was difficult at the time to be thankful that the well cost over $5,000 to drill. But that came under the heading of "be thankful for everything." I was thankful that we had enough funds to pay the bill!) Daily I'm thankful that my fingers can still grasp any object at which I take careful aim, and I'm ever so thankful my eyes can still see clearly, albeit now they must peer through pesky bifocals. Do any of these prayers compensate for any lack of meal prayers?

*Many human-type parents teach their children to pray at mealtime and bedtime because it's good training. I did, too. And my kids spouted their ritual little "Now I lay me down to sleep" and "God bless our food" routines. But they were encouraged to add their own petitions and, personally, I think the Lord was much more interested in that portion of their prayers. The Bible says, **"And when you pray, do NOT use VAIN REPETITIONS as the heathen do, For they think that they will be heard for their many words," Matt. 6:7**. The Lord probably heard no repetitions of my son's special petitions, some of which were...*

<u>At Age 4</u> - "Thank you for windows for little boys to put fingerprints on."

At Age 6 - ". . .help the people with broken legs get crutches" and "help the poor people to get aspirin like the rich people who HAVE aspirin."

...but I'll bet He liked them better than all the "Now I lay me down to sleep" petitions the kid ever parroted.

The Bible always uses the terminology of God being a Father to all who are born in His family through faith in Christ (John 1:12-13). He is a Father that is so interested in each of His children that **"the very hairs of your heads are all numbered"** Luke 12:7 (pluralized). That is INTIMATE knowledge of your children. My kids were lucky if their hair got clipped and <u>combed</u>, let alone <u>counted</u>.

But even though God has that much interest in His children, He never forces any of us to "call home." He DOES make it as easy for us as He can though. Sprint doesn't even offer such a deal:

1. There's no toll charge and no busy signals. He's given us His direct access line which is the name of Christ. **"For through <u>Christ</u> we have access by one Spirit to the Father." Eph. 2:18.** The name of Christ is the ONLY name given in the Bible for us to use as being able to make the connection between God and man. **"...There is ONE mediator between God and man, the man Christ Jesus." I Tim. 2:5.**

What's the hitch? There's ALWAYS a hitch... **"You ask and do not receive, because you ask for wrong things, that you may have pleasure." James 4:3**; and **"...if we ask anything ACCORDING TO HIS WILL, He hears us. I John 5:14.** UNFORTUNATELY, we must request things that God knows are RIGHT for us. I don't always do well here. I'd rather have things EASY, as well as pain free and comfortable, thank you. Many times God must overrule my desires and give me what's beneficial for me so I'll grow spiritually—even if it causes me hard work and some "growing pains."

2. He provides an interpreter to make our mumblings something He can understand: **"...For we do not know what we should pray for as we ought, but the Holy Spirit makes intercession for us..." Romans 8:26.**
3. There's no worry that I'll run out of minutes on my "plan". **"Pray without ceasing..." I Thess. 5:17**; and **"...in <u>everything</u> by prayer and supplication, with thanksgiving, let your requests be made known to God." Phil. 4:6.**

Now, even though God won't force you to have long chats with Him, think how your <u>earthly</u> father would react if you phoned him dutifully every day but only ever said, "Hi Dad. Thanks for dinner!" and hung up. You'd have your father sputtering..."W-A-I-T a minute! Tell me what's happening! I'm INTERESTED in your life. Is there anything I can help you with?" But, of course, the phone would be disconnected and just be going "BUZ—Z—Z—Z—z—z—z..."

....which brings us to one of my quirks. I love getting phone calls from my kids, but the ones I like the best are the ones that AREN'T on Mother's Day or my birthday. Birthday/Mother's Day calls are "HALLMARK" calls...and there's not one person out there who doesn't know what I mean. If I DON'T get a call on those days, I feel TERRIBLY abused and forgotten, yet it bothers me when the calls DO come because I fuss and fume that the kids are calling because society and Hallmark Industries have guilt-tripped them. ("YOU DIDN'T CALL YOUR MOTHER ON MOTHER'S DAY!!?? What kind of schmuck

ARE you!?") I always felt guilt-tripped on those "Hallmark Holidays" as I made my dutiful calls. So, just this year I made a deal with my youngest son. I won't look for a call on Mother's Day or my birthday but, sometimes, he'll call "just because" he cares and knows that I care.

So, if I offend anyone by not praying at every meal, I'm truly sorry, but I DO "call" my Heavenly Father every day and we have long, comfortable chats about the good, the bad, and the indifferent going on in my life — "just because" He cares.

You know, I <u>really</u> don't think He's upset with me.

The Terrible Parable of the Pregnant Neighbor Man

Bryan was 16 months old; Jeff 4 ½ years old when I wrote the following in my diary:

> **"Bryan tumbled down the basement stairs today. I think his little noodle hit every step possible. When I came tearing down the steps to comfort a hurting child, Jeff demanded indignantly, 'MOMMY!! Why didn't you keep an EYE on him?!'"**

Unfortunately, I only had two eyes—but THREE very active children. Many days I felt I had too few eyes allotted to me, and my kids had a couple bumps and bruises to prove it. My diary doesn't say whether I put up any defense on my own behalf or whether, being justly condemned, I simply begged forgiveness. Jeff chastised me as only an indignant 4-year-old can but, fortunately for me, within minutes both of my children had forgiven me and I was back in their good graces.

Forgiveness. What a comforting gift. Sometimes family members refuse to give this gift to each other or eventually reach a limit beyond which they are not willing to forgive. Whatever the reason, when forgiveness is not forthcoming it's heartbreaking, at best, for all involved. My kids, as in the incident above, forgave me often. Of course, there was considerable reciprocation!

Actually, I'm in two families. I was born into my human family by physical birth to my parents; I was born into God's family by faith in Christ (John 1:12-13). As God's child, how much and how often can I expect Him to forgive before He reaches HIS limit? Let's run through a really wacky scenario here.

I've accepted Christ as Savior and therefore have been "born" into God's family, right? Okay. With God keeping a Fatherly eye on me, for a long time I'm a good kid...learn my scripture verses...keep my house neat and tidy...visit sick neighbors...take out the trash...you name it. THEN—one sunny summer day I'm peeking through the fence surrounding the neighbor's yard and I see the neighbor man swimming in his pool. What a BODY!! I start to scheme. I bake cupcakes and take some over to him, giving him a line of bologna, "...just had a few extra...didn't know what to do with 'em...didn't want to throw them out... knew you were all alone since your wife is in the Army in Iraq and you don't get much baked stuff...etc., etc.,"—ad nauseam. He doesn't throw me out, so I stay the night.`

Wouldn't you KNOW it!!! HE gets PREGNANT and comes and tells me about it! Well!! I can't have THIS hanging over my head—what will people THINK!! I arrange for his wife to come home on emergency furlough. She'll think the baby is hers...it'll arrive a little early perhaps, but no big deal. Well, unfortunately, she's so incredibly gung-ho about her duty to her country that she sleeps on the army commander's patio in her camouflage suit instead of going home to be with her husband! She says she can't bear to be having a good time when her buddies are facing a life and death situation on the front lines!! As soon as she can, she splits for Iraq. Women!! Such disgusting creatures!!

What to DO! Only one solution...I arrange for her to be killed behind the lines. You know...a case of "friendly fire"...so incredibly sad, these things. This plan works and news reaches "Body Wonderful" that his wife is dead. He is terribly distraught and grieves. THEN he marries me! WOW—I GOT THE HUNK!!! Of course, our first baby arrives VERY early, but who's counting?

Now, as I count my minor little transgressions here, I find:

1. *Invasion of another person's privacy;*
2. *Lust;*
3. *Adultery;*
4. *Murder;*
5. *Incredibly bad script writing*

Surely God is going to kick my little tail feathers right out of His family, right? WRONG! Seem incredible? Well, if you're familiar with the history of Israel's King David, you'll recognize the scenario as a mangled version of David's sin with Bathsheba (II Samuel 11). Of course, in THAT version, Bathsheba is the one who gets pregnant rather than King David. I'm a bit ahead of medical science with my version, I suppose.

Now King David wasn't a new member of God's family who didn't know the family rules; he deliberately CHOSE to sin—and he picked sins mankind has put on the list of "The Ten WORST Sins." Which, when you think about it, is a strange designation. Personally, I've never seen a list called "The Ten BEST Sins." Check out Proverbs 6:16-19 and you'll find a list of seven things God hates and "a lying tongue" and "a proud look" are listed on the same level as "hands that shed innocent blood," but have you ever heard of anyone getting lynched for being a braggart? (The idea HAS APPEALED to me at times, however.)

God's definition of sin is "to miss the mark." What is this mark? Unfortunately, it refers to "perfection!" No WONDER we humans are sinners...it's been a LONG TIME since I even THOUGHT I was perfect. Now, I'm not saying murder and adultery aren't extremely serious "mark misses," but pride and lying are also serious "misses." Man has a much more lenient definition of "missing the mark" than God does. Unfortunately, we're playing by God's rules, so if you feel the rules should be changed, talk to Him.

So when kids (God's kind or the human kind) "miss the mark," what brings them back into line? Discipline. NO ONE likes discipline. Personally, I used to give my kids to the count of "five" to quit whatever they were doing...and if I was really ticked, I started counting with "four." If they chose <u>not</u> to stop their actions, they were disciplined, THEN they stopped, all was forgiven, and we'd go on from there.

God didn't count to five for David. Instead, Bathsheba's child was taken from them by death and David had numerous other far-reaching family problems that were a natural outworking of his poor actions as a believer, husband and father. David was forgiven when he acknowledged his sins to God, but he still had to live with the results. His life would have been easier had he not gone against God's principles, as will OUR lives be easier if we follow God's rules.

An interesting point here...I and II Chronicles, which is the history of Israel written from God's view of what is important, lists David's sin of numbering the people, but doesn't even MENTION the Bathsheba affair. Rather, God emphasized how David loved Him—which clues you in that God is first concerned about what people think about HIM—then about conduct. You really want to see God's dander get up??? Read about the kings and people who rejected Him...that's when the fur really flew!

David knew God as his Savior and Lord, so God disciplined him but never even CONSIDERED kicking him out of His family. This should be pretty comforting for all of us since I have yet to see a man (or woman) walking the streets shielding his eyes from the glare of his bright, golden halo. (But I know several people who ACT like they've got one. Bet you know a couple people like that too!) Once we're IN

God's family, we're there for eternity, no matter how we mess up and no matter how many times God has to discipline us to keep us following as sheep OUGHTA follow their shepherd:

> **"My sheep hear my voice and follow me and I give them ETERNAL LIFE and they shall NEVER perish; neither can any man pluck them out of my hand. My Father, who gave them to me, is greater than all and no man is able to pluck them out of my Father's hand." John 10:27-28.**

Comforting, huh?!

By the way, this is NOT autobiographical!! Just in case you were wondering!!! It ISN'T possible... YET... for men to get pregnant these days, IS IT????)

The Terrible Parable of the
Professor vs. the Possessor

Well, sir. As I understand your question, you're wondering if God is on this "Christian" preacher's side when he sounds more like a crook than a preacher. Maybe the question should be, "Is this preacher on GOD'S side?" You're assuming that the preacher is acquainted with God because of what? His black suit? Clothes "make the man" we're told. But the guy COULD just be color blind. Is it the "Reverend" he uses in front of his name? Maybe it's because he stands in a little six-sided box, slightly above the congregation on Sunday mornings and quotes Bible verses. That's impressive. But is he really a Christian or just a fake?

Sometimes it's easy to spot a fake. Now, my children are brighter than the AVERAGE children (of course) so my eldest was able to spot a fake at age 5 when Santa visited his kindergarten Christmas party due to the fact that a different "Santa" had listened to his requests the night before. He came home and told me all the gory details:

Jeff: *"Everybody told Santa Claus what they wanted for Christmas, but I didn't."*
Me: *"Why not?"*
Jeff: *"Because he FORGOT me!"*
Me: *"Forgot you? What do you mean?"*
Jeff: *"Well, I already told him what I wanted at the Christmas party LAST night and he didn't remember that I wanted a drum and a real watch, so I wouldn't tell him again!"*

Now, this man had the proper-colored clothing complete with fur trim, a belly that shook like a bowl full of jel—well, lumpy pillows, a highly-respected name, and quoted the verses from Santa's "bible" – "Have you been a GOOD little boy? (Rudolph 2:16) and "What do you want Santa to bring YOU this year?" (Blitzen 3:24). Looked right. Sounded right. And my kid was buying Santa's story UNTIL he talked with him first hand. Then Santa's lofty position took a nosedive as the deception was uncovered, if not exactly understood, by a highly disgusted child.

Now, determining a human's position with God can be a LOT tougher. Some Christians…if they are rebelling and out of fellowship with God…are leading lives that would embarrass a total atheist. I kid you not! Galatians 5:17-21 lists some of the possible horrendous lifestyles.

Other Christians are living nice lives, but hiding their faith under several bushels of neglect and doing absolutely nothing for the Lord. (Having been a rebel, I know whereof I speak on these issues.) If Christians are heavy into rebellion when your life crosses theirs and their rebellion is all you ever see, you may be AMAZED in eternity to find them being ushered past the Pearly Gates into paradise. I can hear the comments now: "Ffftttt! Never thought SHE'D make it!" or "You've GOT to be kidding. He was a Christian? Never darkened the door of the church!"

Then there are people who KNOW they are not Christian and like it that way. They aren't fooling themselves or trying to fool others. No one will bother to double check St. Peter's list for accuracy when these are turned aside. The ones that are scary are the pseudo spiritual humans who have fooled THEMSELVES

50

into believing they are Christians. Sounds ridiculous, doesn't it? Not knowing you're NOT a Christian? Well, I know of a minister who was preaching for about 10 years when he visited another church, heard the gospel, and understood—for the first time—that Christ died instead of him to make him acceptable to God.

I personally knew Paul T., a dear, sweet missionary to the Jews in Ohio. He had decided as a child to be a missionary but was in Bible School before he became a Christian by faith in Christ. He had always been an obedient, "nice" church-going kid and everyone, including HIMSELF, assumed he was a Christian. I know that's what happened since he told me his testimony himself!

This hits REAL close to home with me. I was a "good" girl and went to church and Sunday School EVERY Sunday. I was a "professing Christian." My mouth said all the right words and I believed it in a mental assent way…but my heart really wasn't engaged in the action. Then at age 28 I truly understood—for the very first time—that Christ had to die just for me.

It came as such a SHOCK—this realization of how far I actually had been from God—that to this day I never assume that ANYONE is a Christian just because they go to church or even if they preach from a six-sided pulpit. Matter of fact, those are the people that scare me the most because I fear some of them are just like I was. Do I have any basis for this fear?

"Not everyone who says to Me, 'Lord, Lord' shall enter the kingdom of heaven, but he who does the will of My Father in heaven. MANY will say to Me in that day, 'Have we not prophesied in Your name, cast out demons in Your name, and done many wonders in Your name?' And then I will declare to them, 'I NEVER KNEW YOU; DEPART FROM ME, you who practice LAWLESSNESS.'" Matthew 7:21-23.

People who ASSUME they are Christian—they've done many wonders IN CHRIST'S NAME even—REALLY don't know Him. The good deeds they were doing not only won't count FOR them, they'll actually count AGAINST them. He says the "many wonders" they did in His name were actually evil in His sight (lawlessness). He says, "Get AWAY from me…I don't even KNOW you." Frightening! Who DOES God count as those He knows and who He considers is doing His will?

Then they said to Jesus, 'What shall we do to work the works of God?' Jesus answered and said, 'This is the WORK OF GOD, that you BELIEVE in Him whom He sent!'" John 6:29. *There is a difference between head belief and heart belief!!!! It took me 28 years to find it out.*

Is the good Reverend a "possessor" of Christ through true heart faith or just a "professor"? I haven't the foggiest notion. I'm glad that the Lord, and not ME, will separate the sheep (believers) from the goats (unbelievers) at the judgment seat that's ahead of us. I'd surely have goats in amongst the sheep!

And, by the way, after the Lord's done sorting, I want to find you in among the sheep!!!

The Terrible Parable of God's Righteousness Accounting

Diary Entry - 1967. *"Jeff and his mental math surprise me every now and then. It's Jeff's turn to bring a snack for the twenty-four kids in his kindergarten class tomorrow and he watched and listened as I counted out the cookies he'd need. I got as far as "8" when he piped up with: "Now you just need two more 8's, Mommy."*

I stood there, cookie in hand, dumbfounded, gazing down at a tiny 5-year-old (I had to put elastic in the waistband of size "Slim" pants to keep them from falling off the kid) whose understanding of math was, to me, absolutely amazing!

You see, math and I have never been on civil speaking terms, let alone been friends. So you can imagine my horror when—just when my kids got into the school system—"new" math was introduced. Just looking through Jeff's math book threw me into a mild panic. I had visions of myself ending up cringing and whimpering pitifully in a corner, a broken shell of humanity, defeated by kindergarten math homework. Fortunately, "new" math was just as much of a snap for Jeff as "old" math, so we simply promoted Jeff to "Head Math Tutor" for the younger kids. A major disaster was averted!

That was YEARS ago and, after my kids were grown, I went back into the work force. For several years I worked for two attorneys—making sure before taking the job that I wouldn't need math skills! One loved numbers and whipped through his reconciling tasks with the greatest of ease, but the other one's math un-ability rivaled mine, and he cheerfully admitted it, but he knew better than to ask ME for help. Matter of fact, many times he hurriedly threw his "svelte" 290-pound body over his accounting books if he was working on them when I came into view. He SAID he was doing his exercises, but I've never seen anyone ELSE do exercises by lying on top of their accounting books, so I have a wild suspicion that he tried to save my feelings at the same time he saved those records from my ineptitude. And I think that was really kind, don't you?

I've only found one accounting system that makes sense to me and that's God's. God knew from eternity past that if He used numerals in His accounting system, Jeff would understand, but I would only be able to stand there, cookies in hand, dumbfounded, gazing up at the mighty God, amazed, but definitely not understanding heavenly accounting. So God used the word picture of "accounting," without using any numerals, to get His truth across.

Let's say we can peek into heaven's computers (they MUST have gone modern by now) and pull up C:\Earth\ USA\Vermont\Houghton\Carolyn. Let's skip right past several of the choices on the main menu bearing my name. Surely none of you are interested in such topics as "Evil Tendencies," "Excess Baggage Dragged Through Life," "Milk—Spilled and Cried Over," or "Opportunities—Golden but Wasted." Even if you ARE interested, this is MY parable and I'm gonna pull up what I very well CHOOSE to show you!! It's:

<u>*"Righteousness–Debits and Credits to Account"*</u>
(Selected items of time line only)

Date:	*4-29-40*
Age:	*0 Earth Years*
Activity:	*Birth of baby girl (incredibly cute)*
Righteousness:	<u>*Debit*</u>
Reason:	**"Behold, Carolyn was brought forth in iniquity."** **Psalm 51:5**

Date:	*9-16-50*
Age:	*10 Earth Years*
Activity:	*Smacked living stew out of sister with flyswatter because sister was teasing her. (Sister DESERVED the swatting, but this is Carolyn's record and the swatting did meet with parental approval!)*
Righteousness:	<u>*Debit.*</u>
Reason:	**"For Carolyn has sinned and come short of the glory of God." Romans 3:23.** **"There is none righteous** *(including Carolyn)***, no not one." Romans 3:10**

Date:	*11-18-54*
Age:	*14 Earth Years*
Activity:	*Awarded pin for five years perfect attendance in Sunday School. Works extremely hard at being good in class. Knows all the right answers in SS class and is quite proud of herself.*
Righteousness:	<u>*Debit*</u>
Reason:	**"For Carolyn, being ignorant of God's righteousness and seeking to establish her own righteousness, has not submitted to the righteousness of God. For <u>Christ</u> is the end of the law for righteousness to everyone who <u>believes.</u>"** **Romans 10:3, 4. "Now to Carolyn who works"** *(hard in SS Class to make a good impression,)* **the wages are not accounted as grace but as DEBT. But to anyone who does not work, but <u>believes</u> on Christ who justifies the ungodly, his** *(or her)* **faith is accounted as righteousness." Romans 4:4,5**

Date:	*7-3-68*
Age:	*28 Earth Years*
Activity:	*Head knowledge from childhood hit heart today. Understood by faith that Christ died and rose again to pay for her sins instead of asking her to pay for her sins herself!*
Righteousness:	**<u>CREDITED</u>** *with Christ's righteousness!*
Reason:	**"For with the heart Carolyn <u>believed unto righteousness.</u>" Romans 10:10** *Carolyn is now...* **"in Christ, not having her own righteousness which is by the Law** *(of Moses),* **but...has the righteousness which is from God by <u>faith.</u>"** **Phil. 3:9.**

See THAT!!! Not one numeral to confuse me! God knew from eternity past that someday He'd have to let me into heaven because Christ's righteousness would be credited to my account in 1968. Do you suppose He did away with numbers in "Righteousness Accounting" in self-defense...just so He won't have to throw Himself over His accounting records every time I come into HIS view for all eternity?? N-a-a-a-h!!! W-e-l-l-l-l, maybe.

m-m-M-M-M!
The Terrible Parable of Roast Beast!

(This was written to my husband's niece when she had her first baby.)

Well, girl! How is that baby, growing? Let's see...he's two months old already! Isn't it amazing how fast time flies when I'm not the one changing 20 or so diapers a day! Pretty soon he'll have enough teeth to start the ever-popular gnawing stage where EVERYTHING gets chewed, whether or not it's edible.

As I recall ancient motherhood history, I put meal after meal of nourishing food in front of my children's faces, but my youngest chewed the end of the stereo cabinet anyway. It was just "mouth high" and it seemed quite logical to him to hook his teeth over the edge and gnaw while listening to the music. If he tired of the stereo's flavor, his next choice was a Twinkie or a Ho Ho. Milk, meat and veggies came in last on his "favorites" list but he could always find room for a great tasting watermelon SEED for dessert (he wouldn't eat the red part, of course!). Naturally, he'd try ANYTHING that WASN'T good for him, including recycled gum he found on the street one time and, another time, liquid shoe polish. Despite his terror tactics, I survived his childhood and he mistakenly ate enough nourishing food to grow up with a strong, healthy mind and body just as your baby is beginning to do now.

So kids grow if you can sneak in nourishing food when they aren't looking. So what else is news? Nothing. But the Bible says Christians are supposed to "grow" no matter how young they are OR how old and feisty they get. And speaking of "old and feisty" and of having to "sneak in nourishing food," who should pop into my mind but your Uncle Doug!

Now, Unc was spiritually "born" in a field when he was already kinda old and feisty. (He was only 28, but he got old early in life.)He was out walking in a field, thinking about verses I had "fed" him when it all fell into place for him. But since that made him a spiritual "baby," I expected him to act like the Bible says a newborn spiritual baby SHOULD act:

> **"As newborn babes, desire the pure MILK of the WORD that you may grow thereby." I Peter 2:2.**

He was supposed to have a DESIRE to study the Bible and mature! Well, he didn't! I couldn't understand him. After I was born again I sat and read the Bible by the hour to find out just what it said. I wanted to know EVERYTHING and I wanted to know YESTERDAY! Your Unc seemed content just to BE! For several years his spiritual growth hovered just above the "May-he-rest-in-peace" level.

I tried to sneak in some spiritual food...bought him a Bible that was easier to understand. He was happy to have it and laid it dutifully on the bedside table, never opening it up for a tiny nibble to see if it tasted good. (He did a lot of reading, but all of it was "Twinkies and Ho-Ho's"—nothing spiritually nourishing.) I pointed out biblical doctrines I found exciting...he would nod and agree and gently spit the information back out as though it might possibly contain that disgusting veggie...broccoli! I told him about things happening in the world that showed prophesy was coming to pass just as the Bible predicted...and his eyes would glaze over and I could read in their depths, "She can't fool me. That's creamed asparagus." And he would refuse to swallow.

I gave up. I figured he had decided he PREFERRED to stay spiritually malnourished. It's very possible, you know, for Christians to neglect or refuse spiritual food and the "Spirit section" continues to be weak and useless to themselves and to the Lord. It's definitely not what the Lord wants for His children, just like you wouldn't want your baby's physical growth to be stunted. Can you imagine your baby never growing physically stronger than he is now? He'd never be able to walk, run, or ask for the keys to dad's car! But God doesn't attach strings and make us puppets when we become His. We're allowed control of our actions, growth, and conduct. (Can you imagine what a ruckus Unc would have kicked up had he seen a puppet string dangling near any of his feisty streaks?!)

Then we moved to Vermont and I happened upon a little church and went one night to see what they taught. I LIKED EM! Gingerly, EVER so gingerly, I approached Unc with the suggestion we go to church there once...just once. "Are there PEOPLE there?" your loner-type Unc demanded. Well, I had to admit there were a few. He scowled and asked, "Do I have to TALK to 'em?" I assured him I'd protect him as best I could. He could hide behind my purse or something. We went. He found it TOLERABLE, if not enjoyable. Even thought the sermon wasn't bad, and the people "okay" as long as they stayed F-A-A-R away from him.

Well, to make a long story short, the pastor and Unc became good friends and the mouth of your Unc's mind was pried open long enough for him to taste the scriptures. He found, much to his surprise, they weren't broccoli flavored at all, but "roast beast" and mashed potatoes sandwiched between black leather covers. He found there was HISTORY in there. I had been feeding him doctrine–my idea of dessert–while there was HISTORY to sink his teeth into. Same restaurant–different menu.

Now he sits with his Bible and his reference books and digs out the information on where the Apostle Paul (his hero) went and what he taught as well as what kind of a man Paul was. He thinks the historical book of Acts is a FASCINATING book where, to me, it's mostly spiritual liver.

Amazing Book, that one. It has portions for every taste and it changes the lives of those who study it and grow by it. It's SMART, too. Look what the Bible has to say about itself:

"The Word of God is alive and powerful...sharper than any two-edged sword, piercing to the division of the soul and spirit and the joints and marrow and is a discerner of the thoughts and intents of the heart." Hebrews 4:12.

And it tastes rather like "roast beast" to the stranger ones among us.

The Terrible Parable of the Second Pregnancy

SO!!! You're going to have a BABY!! How wonderful! The Bible says children are a gift from God and **"happy is the man who has his quiver full of them."** *That verse was written LONG before it cost an arm and a leg to raise a SINGLE child, let alone a whole quiver of 'em. So, if you want to be happy with only one or two kids, it's okay with me. I was given three "gifts from God" and one of them had a rather whopper-jawed view of the whole birth process as a diary entry from 1972 years ago reflects:*

> **Bryan, age 6, and a small female-type person, age 8, were having an extremely heated discussion:**
>
> **Female-Type: "I can have a baby if I WANT to!!"**
>
> **Bryan: "NO YOU CAN'T!! If you have a baby before you're married, you know what would happen?!"** *And here he dramatically paused...then, small hand on hip, he vehemently continued,* **"They'd put it RIGHT BACK IN!! You CAN'T HAVE IT!"**

Now, at the tender age of 8, this tiny female may have had a harder time HAVING a baby than Bryan would have had "putting it back," but the thought of either sends rather violent shudders up and down my spine! Where do kids come UP with this incredible knowledge that they dispense so freely and with such conviction?

But their argument brings to mind a couple truths that apply to birth; namely, no one can get into a human family unless he or she is first BORN. Nor can any person born EVER be "put back in." Facts of life. You were born into your family. Bryan was born into mine. Even though Bryan wasn't a "planned" baby, we didn't even CONSIDER trying to "put him right back in." Some impossibilities remain impossible and Bryan will be in my family FOREVER! (And I do LIKE that, by the way—just in case you were wondering.)

Jesus used the illustration of the human birth process to explain to Nicodemus how a man, woman or child is born into God's family by a <u>second</u> *birth...* **("Except a man be born AGAIN, he <u>cannot</u> see the Kingdom of God." John 3:3)...** *that He says is absolutely necessary and which keeps a person in God's family forever. (***"...whosoever <u>believes</u> in Him shall <u>NEVER</u> perish but have everlasting life." John 3:16)**

Now, I'll bet you thought my youngest "gift from God" was the only one in all of history to make such a profound statement as "They'll put it right back in!"– but listen to the question Jesus was asked by Nicodemus, who was a highly respected teacher of the Jewish religion, when Jesus clued "Nick" in that a second birth was essential:

> **"Nicodemus said to Him, 'How can a man be born when he is old? Can he enter a second time into his mother's womb and be born?'" John 3:4**

Bless Nicodemus' confused old heart—I rather hope he never found out that his conversation with Jesus was published and read by millions of people through the ages. Poor guy. It was a big "Kodak Moment"—and not only did he not get the picture, he wasn't even sure how to hold the camera!

*So Jesus explained to him: "**That which is born of the flesh is flesh** (humans can only produce another human into their human family)**...and that which is born of the Spirit is Spirit" John 3:6.** (The Spirit of God has to get in on the act to produce a spiritual "birth" to get us grungy humans into God's family.) If the Bible is true, all of us (including your baby when it's born) need a second pregnancy...a spiritual one...to get into God's family.*

Spiritual pregnancies are similar to human pregnancies. The first pregnancy that produced me was the usual variety—started with a seed; I grew in the dark for nine months; was nourished before birth; and was born with a flourish at the proper time. (Well, ALMOST the proper time. I was late for my own birthday...was due in very early April but refused to appear until April 29th. My uncles wanted my folks to name me "April-Darn-Near-May.")

I was slow in arriving at my "second birth" too. The Bible says those who don't yet understand that Christ died instead of them to make them right with God are "in the dark" spiritually, but that the Word of God is "nourishment" that is fed to them while they're in the dark until they "grow in faith" to the point where they "come into the light" and are born spiritually as "newborn babes in Christ."

Well, my folks trundled me off to Sunday School from the time I was old enough to BE trundled, and there I was fed the Word of God. I went through Catechism and was smug that I knew all the answers. (I was a royal PAIN) Sat through church every Sunday and was fed more of God's Word. When I was older I even TAUGHT Sunday School. No second birth. I stayed in that "womb" for 28 years!

Finally, I started going to a Bible study at a friend's house. One day that friend asked me if I believed Christ died for me. I said, "Yes, I've ALWAYS believed that." But, for the first time, it made sense to me and I had my "Ah HA! Moment." God heaved a B-I-I-G sigh of relief. I'd FINALLY "seen the light" of His truth and was born the second time with a flourish into His family simply by believing and understanding what He'd done for me 2,000 years ago! It has greatly enriched my life.

SO!!! Even before your baby has had its FIRST birthday, my wish for him or her is to have a second "birth day" into God's family – hopefully with a spiritual pregnancy shorter than 28 years!

"Marvel not that I say unto you, you <u>must</u> be born again." John 3:7.

The Terrible Parable of the Student

<u>Diary Entry – September 1971</u>: *"Boy! In just an hour, you'll go to kindergarten for the first time! Isn't that EXCITING?" I enthused to Bryan. He scowled and muttered, "I don't think it's much besighting. I'll have to see if I LIKE it or not first."*

School never did get "besighting" for Bryan. Several days I trundled him off to school at 8:30 only to have him miraculously reappear by 9:30. Seems that when the rest of the kindergarten class would line up and take a hard left turn to go to the music room, he would take a hard right and split for home (that was only a block away from the school). After he realized this procedure wasn't going to fly, "besighted" about it or not, he stayed in school, studied books—when he absolutely, positively HAD to—graduated, and went off to Colorado to mechanics school.

In Colorado Bryan studied how to repair engines. The manual and the teacher both said, "To time an engine, follow steps (a), (b), and (c)." Smart lad that he was, he studied the manual, listened to the teacher, and timed engines by following steps (a), (b), and (c).

Now, suppose Bryan cut all his classes and threw out the instruction manual. BUT!...he <u>sincerely believed</u> that the way to time an engine was to stomp on the brake pedal several times with precisely 75 pounds of foot pressure while the engine was idling and the front windows were rolled half-way down. Sincere belief or not, when the day came to time an engine, he could have stomped every brake pedal ever manufactured into oblivion and—cheeks undoubtedly red with embarrassment—never timed ANYTHING!

God gave man a manual. It gives instructions on how to become His child, how to live a life that is pleasing to Him, and even tells mankind how to obtain rewards made of gold, silver, and jewels that will last for eternity. Often His manual is bound in black leather, is difficult to locate in the home, and is usually covered with a thick layer of dust even though we're advised to...

"...Study to show yourself approved unto God, a workman that need not be ashamed, rightly dividing the Word of truth." II Timothy 2:15.

Bryan studied in order to be a mechanic who wasn't ashamed of his skills. God wants Christians to study His manual so we're not embarrassed by a lack of Christian skills. One of the basic skills a Christian worker should have is the ability to tell others about Christ:

"How shall they believe in Him of whom they have not heard? And how shall they hear without a preacher?..." (Romans 10:14, 15)

...so I TRY to tell people about Christ, but it seems I run into VERY "unbesighted" students. Recently I spoke with a college kid (...anyone under the age of 30 is a "kid" to us old folks) who was quite emphatic that he needed no manual and no teacher to tell him about God...he was quite capable of making up his own mind without any assistance, thank me very much! Interesting!

For YEARS this college student has willingly paid hard, cold cash to listen to professors because he needs to learn about the subjects they teach. He would be <u>horrified</u> if asked to understand any college subject *without having read the manual and without having listened to teachers explain the more difficult aspects. To what end? So he can get a job and make enough money to buy food and clothing for the next 40 years or so. Then he'll get old and wrinkled and <u>D-I-E</u> just like everyone else and it won't matter what he has learned.*

BUT!!! our college student needs absolutely no help to learn about the One who brought into existence the very basis—and created the very theories—of the subjects he's been trying to learn the last 15 years! He'll decide about the Author/Creator of the subjects by himself—without studying, without being taught, and certainly without reading any musty old manual. He was unbiased, though ...didn't just reject the Bible. He graciously included ANY religious book in his sweeping rejection. AMAZING!!

Also odd. He has willingly invested 15 years of his life preparing for a job that will last a miserably short 40 years, but refused to even consider studying or preparing for eternity. And eternity lasts a L-O-T longer than 40 years. When the time comes to test his beliefs in eternity, is our student going to WISH he had checked them out before the lid of his little casket clanged shut?

*The Bible says, **"It is appointed unto man ONCE to die, and after that, the judgment." Hebrews 9:27.** We've only got this lifetime to learn about the roadmap that leads to glory. When the lids of our caskets clang shut we'll be too tired to study and it'll be too dark in there to read anyway.*

Think I'll study for the most important test of my life while I still have time here. How about you?

The Terrible Parable of the Wet Whistle

Little kids are so incredibly DENSE!! Or maybe parents are just difficult to understand. I'm not sure which was the problem 50 years ago when my kid was about three years old, but he caused me considerable frustration one night when...

"...Jeff was already in bed and decided he needed a drink of water. I made a major mistake! I asked him, "Would you be satisfied to just wet your whistle?" The only "wet whistle" he could think of was a plastic one shaped like a bird that warbled when you put water in it and then blew into the bird's "tail." He REALLY felt he should drink from that whistle if he was supposed to be "wetting his whistle." I explained over and over that his "whistle" was his mouth; then he tried to whistle and drink at the same time. He never did understand, and I got no peace until I let him hold the bird whistle with the promise he could "wet it" in the morning."

My diary doesn't say whether Jeff tried to drink from the bird whistle the next morning or not. I HOPE he didn't, but if he did, I probably let him and relied on my grandmother's philosophy of "Ya gotta eat a peck of dirt before ya die!" that she used while raising her nine kids. It took a lot of the pressure out of child rearing.

There's plenty of pressure left in child raising even if you <u>can</u> watch 'em eat a peck of dirt without flinching. Kids "understand tanks" are empty and need to be filled. Kids must learn to understand the foreign language their parents speak (English must sound like absolute <u>gibberish</u> to a newborn), the difference between right and wrong, how to settle a disagreement without the assistance of a 45 Magnum— ALL the small stuff. A wise parent fills their child's tanks with the best human-type information they have available so their child will grow into a responsible adult who understands important things...like the meaning of "wetting one's whistle."

All humans come with an empty "spiritual tank" too. That tank <u>stays</u> empty till the Holy Spirit gets His chance to fill it with God-type information when someone accepts Christ as Savior and becomes God's child to raise spiritually. **(John 1:12-13 and John 14:26)** *God's been trying to fill my tank ever since I understood and believed that Christ died for me and rose again, but either I'm incredibly dense or God is difficult to understand. Whatever the reason, I must cause Him <u>considerable</u> frustration! Jeff didn't understand wet whistles for a while there, but it took me YEARS to understand God's wet frogs. Have you had the frog lesson yet?*

Remember Moses? Moses knocked on the Pharaoh's door way back when and asked if the Israelite slaves could come out to pray. "No WAY!" Pharaoh snarled! (He had an ATTITUDE problem!) Pharaoh wasn't going to let all that cheap slave labor slip though HIS fingers! But God and Moses had attitudes of their own and God sent 10 plagues on the Egyptians to show Pharaoh just who he was DEALING with there! And <u>there's</u> where I got confused. Since the plagues were to show God's tremendous power, why did God choose to have cute little frogs hopping over the land as one of the plagues? Who's afraid of cute little FROGS anyway? Let all that slave labor loose just because <u>frogs</u> hopped around? I don't THINK so!!

Now, I wasn't <u>totally</u> sarcastic about God's choice of plagues. I even approved of a couple of 'em; the water changing into blood—<u>that</u> was good! Death of the first born—VERY dramatic. But there were also the darkness, lice, flies, hail and dying-cattle plagues. They were ok-a-a-a-y, but really not as dramatic as I would expect from my all-powerful God. Why not have the earth open up and swallow Egyptians but

61

spew back out of its depths any stray Israelite who happened to be living, or walking, on the wrong side of the pyramid that afternoon? You know—<u>majestic</u> stuff!

Was there something I was not understanding? Was I trying to whistle and drink water at the same time here?

After about 20 years of confusion on the subject, I finally heard an explanation of the wet-frog saga that made the whole thing sensible. Egyptians worshiped the frog-goddess, Heka, as well as six million or so OTHER deities. (I guess they didn't want to take the chance of leaving any "god" out.) So when the frogs ran amuck in the land, the Egyptians must have thought their own god had run amuck. <u>That</u> puts a different light on a slippery subject.

Water changing into blood? The Nile River was sacred to the god Osiris, who was credited with bringing fertility to the land and life-giving water to the people. When the water was turned into blood, Osiris could only bring death rather than life. Ah HA! A SECOND Egyptian god downed and drowned!

*The plague of Lice? Geb was the Egyptian earth-god. If Geb really were God, he could have controlled the substance comprising his domain, but "**the dust of the land became lice.**" Geb HAD no power and another Egyptian god bit the dust, so to speak. Pun intended.*

The head honcho of Egyptian gods was Ra, the sun-god. Ra was powerless to overcome Jehovah's darkness that He brought on the land. Jehovah had shown the Egyptians that He could flip Ra's light switch permanently to "off."

*And on and on and on...9 plagues...9 Egyptian gods blasted out of the saddle! Then came the 10th plague—death of the first born. According to Egyptian religion, the first-born child belonged to the gods. Jehovah **<u>destroyed</u>** what belonged to the Egyptian gods. The gods could not protect what was supposed to be their own property, let alone the people who worshiped them. That REALLY rubbed salt deep into the wound—so deep that even Pharaoh understood who he was dealing with and let the Israelites go.*

So! Was I incredibly dense or WHAT? Please...be kind when you answer that. I'm sensitive. I've got a lot of empty space in my "spiritual understanding tank" yet that God is working to fill and I'm hoping it will be filled to the brim before it's my turn to travel to my heavenly home.

I pray the same for you.

Index

About the Author

*This photo of us was taken 35 years ago when we were CONSIDERABLY younger
and how I hope we will look when we're both in glory for eternity!!!!*

The author has absolutely no credentials but if you know her, you'll find she has what she calls a "whopper-jawed" sense of humor and this comes out in all her writings. She is a committed Christian whose purpose on this earth is what she calls "being a seed dropper for the Lord." She raised three children who gave her all the ammunition she needed to write these Terrible Parables. She now lives in Vermont and is waiting for the Lord to call her home so she can rejoin her husband who graduated to glory in March of this year.

Printed in the United States
By Bookmasters